BORN *into* HELL

Ana Waterman

ISBN
978-0-578-54187-7 (paperback)
978-0-578-54771-8 (digital)

Copyright © 2018 by Ana Waterman

All rights reserved. No part of this publication may be reproduced, distributed, or transmitted in any form or by any means, including photocopying, recording, or other electronic or mechanical methods without the prior written permission of the publisher. For permission requests, solicit the publisher via the address below.

Printed in the United States of America

To Opee and Teddy

My dear brothers and silent co-authors.

We sustained, yet survived
The atrocities that occurred in our house.
Only we know what truly happened there
and are willing to tell about them today.

Yes, we were *victims* back then,
Some of us are *victors* today!

Contents

Acknowledgments...vii
Introduction.. viii
The Family.. ix
1 Her Hell Ended...1
2 My First Memories and Bingo's Hell......................9
3 No Bed of Roses at the Flower Nursery.................22
4 More Nursery Rhymes.......................................35
5 Existing on Moffia Road....................................49
6 She Left Us Before She Was Gone.......................64
7 Trying to Climb Out of Hell /First Grade..............77
8 Maybe There Is a Heaven /Second Grade............101
9 Turning Up the Fire of Hell /Third Grade............108
10 Hell on Navajo Road/Fourth Grade...................129
11 Hell on Hale Street..135
12 Will the Hell Ever Come to an End..................145
13 Released from Hell Still Smoldering..................156
14 Life after Death..189
Epilogue...193
Goodbye from Me to You...................................196
Today..197

Acknowledgments

Mildred Nelson Holmes, author, *Poor Orphan Trash*

This book would not have been possible without the generous and loving help and support from my writing coach, modeling instructor, special friend and mentor, Mildred Nelson Holmes. She and I lived under similar circumstances and are willing to tell about it today. She knows me for who I truly am, and from whence I came. Only a Southern writer as she could empower and propel me to the deep-seated truth as written in these pages. Her talents enabled and motivated me to tell it all from the heart.

Her incredible diligence in editing my many pages of scrambled English grammar was amazing.

To my husband, Ralph

For his loving devotion to me, constant patience with me while writing, his purity of soul, and for his love of God.

God Almighty

Finally, I would like to thank God for urging me to share my story. He was with me all the way during those bad days—even when I didn't realize it.

Introduction
Hello from Me to You

I have been asked: "Why do you feel the need to relive the atrocities that you and your siblings suffered as children? Why do you want to write about such heinous events?"

My only answer is: If I do not write it down, our story will go untold, and it will be unnoticed forever.

Those little children from the past will never get their closure. They will have suffered for no good reason. Can we *please* make something good out of something terrible?

This little book does not have a storybook theme in which to follow. Please do *not* expect to read it as such, for I am not a professional author. This book is merely a collection of the memories that remain with my brothers and me. We are willing to share them with you.

According to a study published in 2009, *Clinical Psychology Review* examined sixty-five studies in twenty-two countries, and using the available data at that time found that 19.7 percent of females and 7.9 percent of males are victims of child sexual abuse. The American Psychiatric Association states that "children cannot consent to sexual activity with adults."

Research factors prove that child sexual abuse often occurs alongside other confounding variables, such as poor family environment and physical abuse.

In our family, we had all the makings of a perfect storm: *Illiteracy*, which leads to poverty. *Poverty*, which leads to violent behavior and disrespect for life and persons, included in this is sexual abuse. *Violence* can escalate into family atrocities. *Atrocities* . . . heinous crimes committed against my brothers, sisters, and me. We lived through it and suffered from it and yet we survived.

No one ever knew what went on at our house.
Well, Mama and Daddy, I'm going to tell on you!

The Family

Fob and Mama
    Children in order of age:
Robby
Ellen
Opee
Theo
Baby John---escaped from his hell of leukemia at the age of six months.
The lucky one.
Tooty
Teddy
Ana---the little wild rose, the middle child. She lived with two daddies--but was not fathered by either one.

Fred and Mama
    Children in order of age:
Mary
Junior
Ginger

1.

Her Hell Ended

I was awakened by the loud, annoying ringing of the old black telephone that rested in the hallway of my aunt Sweetie Pie's lovely home. Aunt Sweetie Pie answered it. I sat straight up in my cousin's bed, fearing the news that phone call might be bringing. Aunt Sweetie Pie started sobbing. My worst fears were right! She was dead! Uncle Alfred, in his striped boxer underwear, came to console Aunt Sweetie Pie. We all started crying without being told the news. My pretty cousin, whom we called Cricket, hugged me as we cried together in her bed. Aunt Sweetie Pie entered the bedroom; she hugged me as she sobbingly said, "Suga, your mama just died." I screamed even louder than before, "Oooooooh! Nooooo!"

Meanwhile, across town, in a dirty little duplex, there lay asleep my three Marine brothers and filthy Fred--my stepdaddy. When the telephone rang, my eldest brother, Robby, answered it. His response to the others was, "Well, boys, you've just lost the best friend you'll ever have in this lifetime."

The only comment Opee could make was, "I'll go get Teddy." He needed to be alone in his sorrow.

I was told Fred turned into an ugly, babbling, squalling idiot when he heard the sad news.

It was six-thirty on Sunday, August 19, 1962.

Only one week of illness had passed, and now it was all over. The doctors could do nothing to save her. It was a new and strange disease; the doctors in Mobile, Alabama, had never seen before. They called it creeping paralysis in those days. Despite the fact that seven doctors looked at her, time was not on her side.

I was eleven years old when my mama died; I wanted to die with her.

This is the story about how a child can live in the midst of hellacious surroundings and still survive. It is a hell-of-a-thing to live with!

The beginning of the end, all started on a sunny Saturday morning, August 11, 1962. Mama had been having severe headaches all day. She sent me walking to the nearby store to buy Goodies pain relievers. I made several trips that day for the same purpose. She continued to wash clothes on an old ringer-type washing machine and hang them outside on the rusty clothesline. Her head continued to hurt badly, then her hands started tingling. Next, her back started to hurt, and then it went numb. I thought she was having a bad case of the Mulley-grubs, or maybe it was the nervous breakdown that she was always saying she was about to have. Whatever was her problem, I was for sure, walking on eggshells that day!

Mama never went to the doctor unless it was to have a baby delivered, or maybe once for gallstones surgery. The point is, Mama must have been really sick for her to go to a doctor. She called the doctor that evening, and he said to meet him at his office.

We all loaded up in the old Studebaker and took her. All four of us kids plus Fred waited in the car for Mama to come out of her after-hours office visit. The doctor gave her a prescription and told her if she wasn't any better to call him in the morning. That night, on the way home, I could tell Fred was irritated. He was mad because he had a special trip to Nashville planned for the following weekend; Mama getting sick spoiled it. We stopped by the drugstore, Mama went in and got her prescription filled. Then she came back to the old dusty green car, which was packed with us four filthy little kids and her stinky, greasy husband.

Later that night, Mama laid on the couch, where she usually slept. I sat with her head in my lap as I combed her hair. She was falling asleep as the drugs were taking effect. I started crying, but I did not want her to know. I had a real keen feeling that I was about to lose my mother, but I was only eleven years old, what did I know? She wasn't a perfect mother, but she was all that I had. When I could tell she was asleep, I slowly and quietly "tip-pi-toed" off to my bed, where my three younger siblings were sleeping. One of them had already peed in it, so I slept on the floor. There I continued to cry and prayed for God to save my mother.

The next morning, Mama was not any better. In fact, she was worse; she could hardly walk. She called the doctor, and he said to meet him at the hospital. I cried as I ironed her tattered robe, that she never wore. I knew that ironing her robe would be the last thing I would ever do for my mama. As Mama was leaving our tiny duplex, her last words to me were:

"You take care of the little ones now and don't let 'em play in the street, 'cause they might get run over and killed by a car. You be their Little Mama."

I said, "Yes, ma'am. I love you." I watched as she slowly hobbled out the door, off the front porch, and into the car, with no help from Fred. I was crying, but I didn't want her to see. I was afraid she might worry about me. That was the last time I saw her alive. I took a long, hard look at her as the car pulled away. I cried for several hours after she left. I knew . . . I just knew what was going to happen.

I also did exactly as she had instructed me to do,

"take care of the little ones," probably to the point of being bossy, should you ask the little ones.

Later that afternoon, Fred came home with chicken that he fried for our dinner. As he was cooking, he said he thought Mama was just faking her illness because she didn't want him and Opee to go on their trip to Nashville the following weekend.

I thought that was a mean and insensitive statement for Fred to make because I knew Mama was genuinely sick. I felt if Fred had really loved Mama, he wouldn't have said that. He should have been more concerned about her getting well and less concerned about his damn ole trip!

The next day, we went to stay with Mama's sister, Aunt Sweetie Pie. She had a lovely, clean house in the country. She was sweet to us. My cousin, Cricket, was fourteen years old and could cook. Cricket cooked breakfast, which was mostly scrambled eggs, cottage cheese, and milk. I had never had these delicacies. Cricket also prepared dinner because Aunt Sweetie Pie worked outside the home.

I loved staying with this wonderful, decent family. We got a bath each night. Also, we got to sleep in a clean, warm, and dry bed. None of Aunt Sweetie Pie's beds smelled of stale pee, like ours. I slept with my cousin, Cricket. I always thought she was so grown-up and proper. She had pretty red, curly hair that she usually pulled back into a long tight ponytail. She liked rock-'n'-roll music and had a scrapbook of movie stars that she let me look at, if she was with me. She was sweet to me and treated me like I was her little sister. I liked that.

I was a tomboy, so I loved to play ball with my boy cousins. I was good at it. I could run fast and occasionally; I could hit the ball hard. Donny was my age. He was kind to me too. He let me play in his tree house. I loved it there because it was up high where you could see everything. The birds sang louder up there, and the air was fresher; the clouds were closer. Life was just better in that big ole tree house. I went there daily, with or without Donny. I made it my own personal tree house. It was my private getaway for a couple of weeks.

On Tuesday of that week, Aunt Sweetie Pie bought us four little ones a brand-new suit of clothes so we could go visit Mama in the hospital. But for some odd reason, Aunt Sweetie Pie decided not to take us to visit her. She said we had gotten our clothes soiled, and we couldn't go and let Mama see us looking like that. In retrospect, I think Mama must have taken a turn for the worse, and Aunt Sweetie Pie thought it was best that we do not see her in that condition.

Wednesday was Mama's birthday. August 15, 1962, she turned forty five years old. She had a weird dream that night; she shared it with her hospital roommate. She had always claimed to have ESP, but there was no definitive proof of such. However, things would happen from time to time, and she would know they were going to happen before they actually *would happen.* On this particular occasion, she dreamed of being underwater, unable to breathe, looking up at others, unable to speak to anyone, yet she was still alive. That was a very troubling dream, indeed.

Thursday of that week, Mama's lungs started to get paralyzed. She could not breathe. She was placed inside an iron lung machine.

Later in life, I was told while she was in that iron lung machine, she was very afraid---afraid of dying. She looked like a caged animal, with wide-opened eyes---begging for someone to help her---to save her. In retrospect, I am glad now, (that as a child), I was spared from seeing Mama in that condition. I don't think I could have handled it. The casket was bad enough!

Friday, while in that iron lung machine, Mama started mouthing out some words. Because she could make no noise with her voice, a person who could read lips was brought in to interpret what she was trying to say. Mama was asking for her Holiness Preacher from many years past to come and pray for her. He did. After talking and praying with her, he said Mama accepted Jesus as her Savior.

One of those days during the week, my eldest brother, Robby, came home from the Marines, as did our other Marine brother, Theo. My sister Ellen had gotten in touch with the proper authorities and advised them Mama was about to die and could they please send our brothers home to say good-bye to her on her deathbed. As for us four little ones, we had no idea. However, I knew in my heart that it was the end, from that very first Saturday morning trip to the store to get those pain relievers.

Then, the dreadful phone call came that Sunday morning!

The rest of that Sunday, I cried hard and long while in that tall, sturdy, oak treehouse. I fussed at God and questioned his judgment in the matter. How could he do such a horrible thing to me? Salty tears and mucus were swallowed so much that I threw up frothy foam several times. I wrote a statement about what had happened that day. I still have that piece of tattered paper from Cricket's scrapbook. With my bad penmanship, I put my emotions on paper and would read them for years to come.

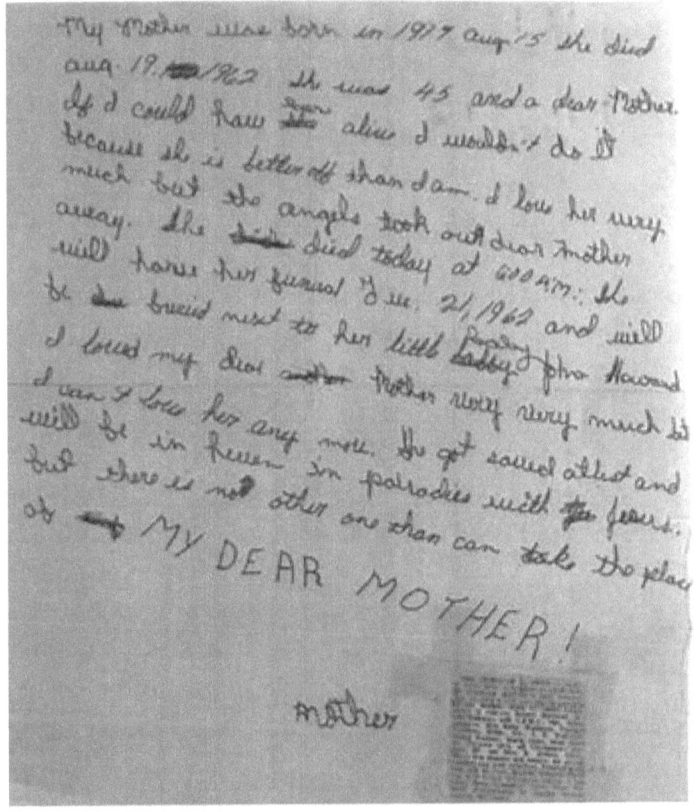

My scrapbook writing on August 19, 1962

Previously, I mentioned Mama had a dream, and she shared that dream with her hospital roommate. The Monday after Mama died, that roommate came back to visit Mama. She was told that Mama had died on Sunday. The lady asked how she had died. The nurse told her that Mama had died in an iron lung machine, and her heart had failed. The nice lady shared Mama's dream. It makes a person wonder about that dream of being underwater, looking up, and not being able to speak, doesn't it? Do you believe in ESP?

The day that Mama died, she was released from her hell here on earth. I too, was released from the hell that she put me through while she was living here.

So, when she was released, I was released. I can't help but wonder if she left this earth only to be placed into a bigger, worse hell somewhere else for the atrocities, which she committed here on this earth against her children. I would like to think not. It is not for me to judge.

"Judge not, that ye be not judged" (Matt. 7:1).

As a child, it matters not how despicable or sorry your mother is; you still love her, because she is the only mother you have and the only one you know. You look up to her for love, guidance, support, and protection. Sometimes, a child gets none of the above, as it was in my case. However, when that mother dies and is gone forever, all hope of *ever* obtaining love, guidance, support, and protection have *vanished forever* . . .

she has taken it all with her.

It was soon after my mother's passing that I realized that a heart can be broken to the point of almost dying—so broken and full of pain, you can't wish death into existence for yourself. *You are dead on the inside*, but that old heart just keeps on beating, and beating, and beating. *Dead on the inside, yet you are still alive on the outside.*

So, you must keep on going and pretending to be alive . . . come hell or high water!

My name is Ana, and this is my story.

2.

My First Memories and Bingo's Hell

This little book is merely a recording of only a few of the unspeakable atrocities that my brothers, sisters, and I endured while growing up in the 1940s, 50s and early 60s in Mobile County, Alabama. The stories told are not necessarily in chronological order. Some of the childhood abominations that are mentioned are *not* for entertainment purposes. It is my hope that this little book will send a powerful message to the victims of domestic violence and child molestation.

My message is this: No matter what has happened to you in your past, you can choose to either be a *victim*, a *victimizer*, or a *victor* for the rest of your life.

I refuse to place blame on others or make excuses. I have chosen to be a *victor!* Your choice is up to you.

Because this book is going to be the story of my humble beginnings, I shall begin by stealing a few select words from:

David Copperfield
by Charles Dickens

> *"To begin my life with the*
> *beginning of my life,*
> *I record that I was born."*

Now I, Ana, do not remember the auspicious occasion of my birth, but I should think my mother did.

My very first memory was when I was around two or three years of age. It was late in the afternoon, and I had just awakened from a nap. I stepped out of our home, which was something that looked like a bus. I learned later it was an old streetcar that had been dragged onto a flower nursery. The man whom I thought was my biological father worked at the flower nursery as an overseer; therefore, we could live there for free. We had no running water, only an outside faucet. The streetcar served as a make-do mobile home for a family such as ours, seven children and two parents.

That afternoon, as I stepped out of that rusty, rundown streetcar, I found my mama and asked her where my red dress was. I must have dreamed that I had a red dress. She did not know what I was talking about; therefore, she ignored me. To this day, I can still see that pretty little thing. I have no idea where I dreamed of such a pretty dress. To my knowledge, I only had one dress to my name and one pair of hand-me-down brown shoes. I know this from old family pictures.

It was late in the afternoon, as the sun was setting. "Poor Old Kaw-Liga" was playing somewhere on a nearby radio. It wasn't our radio, because we had no radio. The song went like this:

> Poor ole Kaw-Liga,
> He never got a kiss.
> Poor Ole Kaw-Liga,
> He don't know what he missed.
> Is it any wonder
> That his face is red?
> Poor ole Kaw-Liga,
> That poor old wooden head.

This song was about a wooden Indian that stood outside a trading post. He was in love with an Indian princess doll in the antique store. He never could tell her that he loved her, for obvious reasons; therefore, he missed out on love.

What a sad song! Isn't that the way life is sometimes?

Some people just can't say "I love you;" therefore, a whole world of warmth and happiness is never known. We children realized this later in life when we looked back and remembered that we never heard those three little words from our parents, "I love you." How sad. It didn't have to be that way.

This is also true today in our personal relationships. Sometimes, we choose not to be close to someone or open to someone and admit that we love them. It is so easy, yet so hard to say those three little words, but what a soothing, blessing it is to receive them. If we all knew how painful it was *not* to hear those three little words, we should say them all day long to everyone that is near and dear to us. Life would be so much better for all if we did.

While living in that meager existence, I remember being happy, because I knew nothing else. My next older brother, Teddy, and I played together with whatever we could find. Usually, we would run on top of the lower glass hothouses, where we were not supposed to play. One day, I fell through the glass and cut a gash in the arch of my foot. I needed stitches, but that was not an option for our family. Mama wrapped my foot in an old diaper type of rag to keep out the dirt, then I got a whipping for breaking the glass.

A nearby, red outhouse was there for use when the need arose. Teddy and I would go into it occasionally to scare ourselves. We would investigate that stinky, horrible hole and wonder what it would be like should we ever fall into it. We thought that hole must be where hell begins!

Our family shared the use of it with the other workers from the flower nursery. I can still remember the stench of that red, one-holer outhouse with the Sears-Roebuck catalog that was used as toilet paper.

Teddy and I played all over the flower nursery. There was a big, beautiful magnolia tree with all sorts of trash, broken glass, and tar paper piled under it. We could find all kind of things to play with from that pile. One day, while rummaging through the garbage, I picked up a green snake. I screamed and ran away. Teddy, being the brave young man of four years old, went over, picked it up, and let it wind around his fingers and hands. I had never seen a snake before, but for some reason, I knew snakes were not something a girl should mess with. Snakes must be a boy thing, I concluded.

Teddy and Ana

Author's Warning

The continuation of this chapter is *not* for the faint-hearted. Stop reading now, if this describes you!

This part I, Ana, do not remember, however, my older brother, Opee told me about these events much later in our lives. I debated whether to share them with you, my readers. These events are true, sad, and deplorable. To gain the full effect of the story of my life, you must begin to know our biological parents.

This is verbatim from a letter Ana received later in life from Opee.

Robby, our oldest brother, had a dearly beloved dog named Bingo. Bingo was a small dog, mostly white with large brown blotches. Sadly, he passed away. How did he pass away? The flower nursery owner, Mr. Swatty, had purchased some young geese to eat the grass around flowering plants. Every evening, the geese would come back to a screened-in pen for the night. One night, I walked past the pen, I heard a commotion; there I saw our family dog Bingo, attacking the geese. He had crawled under the chicken wire and was killing the geese as fast as he could.

I got Bingo out of the pen. I took him back home and told Dad what had happened. He tied Bingo under the streetcar/house and told us, "don't say a word 'bout dis to nobody." We didn't.

I'm sure when frog-faced Tom Swatty saw all his dead geese, he figured out that one or both of our yard dogs had done the dastardly deed.

In about a week, Dad untied Bingo and Puff, our other dog, from under the streetcar/house. It was a few days when Bingo became violently ill. It was apparent to us that Tom Swatty had sneaked down to our place and left poisoned meat.

It was sad watching Bingo die. That idiot, we called Dad, made it worse by using an old home remedy for a poisoned pet. Warm-up bacon dripping pour the mess down the dog's throat, and make him vomit up the poison. As if Bingo wasn't in enough misery, that finished him off. He died a few minutes later. I buried him close to our home. About a week later, Puff met the same fate. The geese killing and dog poisoning were never mentioned between the two families.

The Continuation of Opee's Story

Now that I'm on the subject of Bingo and Puff, here's a horror story for you—as if I haven't told you enough already. Sometime in 1952, I learned the hard way what castration means. The bastard, Fob, (Dad), decided that Bingo and Puff were copulating (not his word) with female dogs, and he needed to "fix 'em."

I asked Mom what castration meant and if it would hurt Bingo. She assured me it would be painless, and the dogs would be better after it was over. What a damn lie!

On the dinner break the next day, Robby got Bingo. Dad had Robby to hold his mouth closed. Theo and I held his feet. I was horrified and nauseated, seeing Dad squeeze Bingo's testicles. Bingo tried to scream, but Robby kept his mouth closed. Then Dad sliced through a testicle. The way he was squeezing them, the testicle ruptured. I was so damn weak I could barely hold Bingo's legs.

Then more torture began. Instead of cutting through the cord that the testicle was attached to, he began scraping the blade up and down saying that would make the cord curl up when it broke, otherwise, the dog would bleed to death.

Then the same procedure with the second testicle. Why in the hell did the testicle have to be sliced open? I'll never know. It did a lot to poor Bingo's misery.

After Puff watched what Bingo went through, it was a few days before he could be lured to his doom. I begged off on that one. I cried like a baby and got Mom to tell Dad not to make me go through that again. I'm surprised he gave me a pass. While Puff was getting put through hell, I kneeled by a bed and put a pillow over my head. All I could hear was Puff scream.

So, there you have it: a small glimpse at the two people that we called Mama and Dad. A man and woman who were first cousins when they married. Both of which were violent in nature and fed off one another. They hated one another, and they took it out on their poor innocent children in beating frenzies. If two people could do such horrific actions to poor innocent, helpless animals; what *could,* and *would* they do to their children? As this story unfolds, you will learn that after the severe beatings, most of the time us children needed medical attention, but it was never received.

Ana sitting with Bingo in the background

*"The older ya get, the bigger the
beatings get . . .
In the words of my brother Opee.*

I can't tell you how many times Ellen would get whipped just because she wanted to get the last word in when arguing with Mama. I have seen Ellen get switched on both of her legs until they were cherry red. Mama would tell Ellen, "Ellen, if you will shut up and quit trying to get in the last word, I'll quit whopping you!"

With barely an audible mumble . . . a sound, which I cannot spell . . . Ellen would mouth off again, then the whipping would commence. You could tell that Ellen's legs were in a great deal of pain, but she was so intent on proving a point, that she couldn't back down. I suppose the point she was attempting to make was, "I'm tougher than you. Lay it on me, Mama. I can take anything you can dish out!" Eventually, Mama would give up. Ellen would win . . . sometimes. Ellen was growing up and getting too old to be whipped. She was growing tired of the abuse, and vehemently expressed her disapproval of such wrongful mistreatment.

Ellen was fifteen when she got her last beating. It happened like this . . . from the memory of Opee.
It was 1951.

Ellen was fifteen years old and about a month away from marrying Skeeter Couch. She was beautiful and almost a full-grown woman.

I, Opee, was eleven years old. Robby was seventeen, Theo was nine, Tooty was four, and Teddy was fifteen months old. Baby sister, (Ana), was about a month old.

All-day, Mama and Ellen had been going at it—with a war of words. Finally, Mama said, "I give up on you, Ellen, but when your daddy comes home from work today, I'm going to let him have you and see if he can't shut you up with his chap belt."

Hearing that, I knew it was going to be very bad for Ellen. It didn't matter that she was almost a full-grown woman.

Sure enough, when Fob and Robby walked in the house, Mama said, "Fob, I've had hell out of Ellen all day. She is too big for me to whop anymore, so I want you to get your chap belt and learn her to mind me!"

Fob took the chap belt off the nail on the wall. Ellen's eyes widened!

Mama told Robby, Theo, Tooty and me to, "Go somewhere else, you don't need to see this."

She didn't have to tell us twice, out we went. As we walked away, we could hear Fob talking to Ellen. She back talked to him. We were a good distance away when the beating started. We could hear the leather connecting with her skin. Each blow got louder and louder. After six or eight licks, Ellen finally screamed an animal-like sound. It was too late for her, the blows kept right on falling, and she kept on screaming. A feeding-frenzy had begun. Fob seemed to be enjoying every minute of it. He always did.

It was as if his testosterone was getting higher, and he was getting sexually aroused from the act of beating her. It makes one wonder if this could have been a prelude to his sex act, later with Mama. Who knows what a sick mind can conjure up?

The beating finally ended, and Mama called us back into the house. Ellen was sitting straight up at the dinner table bench, her hands were folded in her lap, clasped very firmly. Her shrieking had stopped, now hatred had taken its place. All her exposed skin was blistered. Her bruises were coming up in a dark blue and black color on her back. We could see this from her half torn-off blouse. Her eyes were full of rage as she squinted them and glared around the room, occasionally glancing back at Fob and Mama. She was mad as hell, and we could all tell it. Her lips were pursed tightly together as if to say, *"If you ever do that to me again, I will get back at you . . . if I don't kill you first!"* Although no words were audibly spoken, we knew what she was thinking. We had all been there before. It was lucky for Fob this was her last beating; for the older and bigger we children were getting, the harder it was for us to accept his harsh abuse and treatment.

We felt sorry for her, but we kept our mouths shut!
Oh well! That was our lives back then.

So why do you think my sister Ellen made such a hasty decision to marry at the age of fifteen? She got married to get away from two abusive, crazy parents who didn't know when to stop punishing and beating their children for no good reason!

When Ellen married Skeeter Couch, they too lived on the flower nursery grounds for free, because Skeeter worked there. Unbeknownst to Ellen, she had married one of the meanest men that ever lived. He was just as bad as Fob, but she didn't know it! She married not out of love, but to get away from the abuse she was enduring while living with our mama and Fob. She wanted to date another young man, but Fob demanded she go out with Skeeter Couch. She stepped out of the skillet and into the fire! Hell never ends, the fire just gets hotter!

Their short time of dating ended quickly in marriage. Skeeter was not only mean but sleazy and crude. He thought it was funny to beat their small toddlers just for entertainment. He would knock them down just to see them crawl back to him and beg him to stop, then he would laugh in a devilish way. He often beat Ellen, sometimes choking her to the point of near-death. He would pull out chunks of her hair, not to mention knocking out some of her teeth!

After suffering six long years of marital disparage and perverse harsh treatment from Skeeter, Ellen eventually left him in the dark of the night. It was only five days after she had delivered their third baby, and Skeeter was demanding sex from her. Ellen was not ready for sex, nor was her body; she still had stitches from the delivery. Skeeter was forcing himself on her as usual. He started jerking out her stitches with his big, fat, nasty fingers. As a way of escape, she told him she had to go to the outhouse.

When she left their shack, she just kept walking through the woods. Walking through the darkness of night, and walking, and walking until she reached the safety of another house. When she finally reached the neighbor's house, she was weak and bleeding profusely from her vagina; blood was running down both legs. There she was welcomed in and cared for. There she was safe, and she rested for the night. She left Skeeter and her three small children, including her infant, for her own safety. She never went back to Skeeter.

Ellen had a survivor's spirit. She had taken abuse all her life, and now she was to take it no more! Ellen knew if she had not gotten away from Skeeter, one of them would have wound up dead. She made the right decision.

There was no way for her to take care of her three little children by herself. Ellen had no job and no place to live. Therefore, Mama and Fob helped take care of them for a while. Eventually, Skeeter remarried, and the children went back to live with him. At that time, the three children's hell started all over with his abuse.

Ellen continued to struggle to make a living on her own. She finally landed a job as a drugstore soda jerk. She lived in a nearby, one-room apartment, where she could walk to work daily. A young woman with little education had a hard time making a living in the 1950s. If she kept her mouth shut, she could depend on her beauty to open doors. However, when she opened her mouth, it validated her white trash background, and it sometimes closed those doors.

Eventually, she learned to use her beauty wisely, shut her vulgar mouth; and she found a good man who would love her, despite her white trash background. However, she lived through a great deal of hell all her life before she found her peaceful end. She had no one to show her the way to a proper, decent way of life in her early years. She had to figure it out on her own. It was a long, slow process of trial and error. She lived to be sixty-six years old.

3.

No Bed of Roses at the Flower Nursery

Now I must continue the story of my life with the continuance of my life before my life began.
This part, I do not remember, nor was I involved.

Much gratitude goes to my elder brother Opee, for writing his memories of our poor white trash family and how our brothers and sisters survived the ordeal brought on by our ignorant, partially mentally ill parents.

The stories in this chapter are not for those with a weak stomach or a person who cannot bear to read of the grotesque. I am sorry to say this is truly an ugly story, one that will seem absurdly distorted. It is true in every detail.

As the author, I had to hold my nose and place a bag over my head as I typed these stories. *Consider yourself warned.*

Stories from Opee
Paraphrased by Ana

We were living at Little Wild Wood Flower Nursery where Dad, whom I shall refer to henceforth as Fob, was a laborer. The reason for referring to him by this name is because he was by no means considered to be a daddy to any of us children. Fob had only attended first grade for a few days. There, his formal education ended. He came home from school one day soon after beginning first-grade and told his mama that the boys were making fun of him. His mama got mad and vowed that no one would make fun of her boy! So, she told him, "Ya don't have ta go ta school no more." From then on, he didn't.

With less than a first-grade education, being a laborer was all he could do to earn a living. However, with a house full of hungry children and a pregnant wife to feed, life was tough for a man back in those days. I guess he never figured out what made his wife keep popping out those "young'uns." Our mother didn't like it any more than he did.

They were first cousins when he dragged her off her horse or mule that fateful Sunday afternoon and raped her. There was another story of how Fob came to church that Sunday, not looking for religion, or Jesus, but for sex. It doesn't matter whichever story was the truth. Mama got pregnant that day anyway, at the age of fifteen. Grandmama noticed about seven months later that Mama's stomach was not getting fat because of "baby fat." She asked who the father was, and Mama had to fess up and say it was her cousin, Fob. Quickly, there was a shotgun wedding.

By the time Mama was sixteen, she and Fob were married with a baby very close to being born. In April of that year, it was time for the delivery. What a horrible day that was for Mama! Fob paid a midwife $5 to deliver the baby in a hot, one room, dirt-floored shack. The woman tried for over a day to get the baby out with no luck. The only thing that saved the baby and Mama's life was when Fob's sister just happened to stop by to visit. She blew up when she saw what was happening. Fob's sister cussed him out for everything she could think of. Then she immediately went to town and got a doctor to come and deliver the baby. The doctor had the forceps necessary to pull the baby out of the birth canal. Fob reluctantly paid the doctor $15 for his services.

No one ever said it at the time, but it was thought that Fob secretly wanted Mama and the baby both to die. Then he would be rid of them both. In retrospect, it might have been better for all had it happened that way. The baby boy was named Robby. Seven other children followed rapid fire, one after the other. One of our baby brothers died at six months of age with leukemia. We called him Baby John; he was the lucky one.

That left seven children that would, unfortunately, be born into hell and into this poor white trash family. I, Ana, was child number seven of the living; they called me Baby Sister.

Baby John was the first baby born in 1944 in Mobile County, or so we were told. He was child number five that Mama birthed. He was sick from the very first day of his life. Mama took Baby John to faith healer after faith healer, asking them to lay hands on her baby boy and pray for his healing. There was no cure for leukemia in those days. It truly would have been a miracle had he survived. Looking back, it seems that it was better for him to die. Poor Mama! She would cry for days upon days on her knees for God to heal her baby. It was not to happen. Then after only six months of life on this earth, the day came when our little angel baby died. Mama went crazier than ever before and screamed, "Why did you take my baby, God?" She never got over losing that one baby. She would sit and stare at his picture and sometimes cry, even years later. Although she had ten other children, losing that one meant more to her than all the other ten children combined, so it seemed. Baby John was the lucky one; he didn't have to go through the hell the rest of us had to go through. He had endured a hell of his own at the tender age of six months.

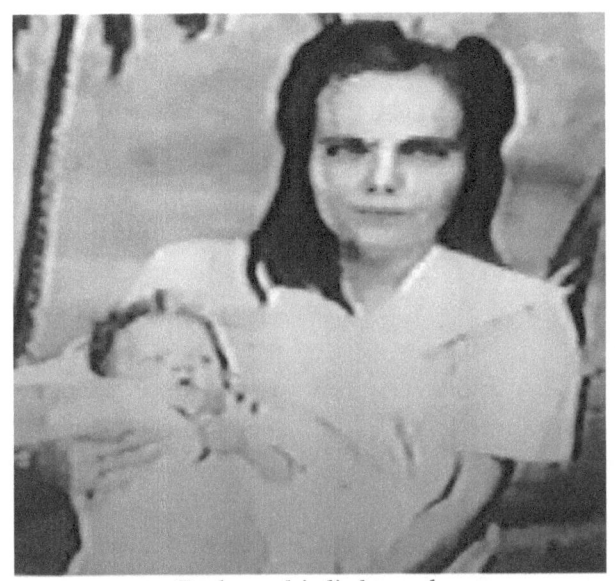

God rest his little soul.
Mama and Baby John

*Opee remembers the day he nearly killed Theo
In 1945. It happened this way:*

I, Opee, was about five years old, and Theo was around two and a half years old. Robby and some of his friends were playing a dangerous game. They had a dry, long, reed shaft. They sharpened one end to a point and threw it at a stack of small boxes. Since Theo and I were small, we couldn't play the game. When the big boys stopped playing, Theo and I ran to get the spear; I got there first. Theo, being defiant, was mad because I got there first. To keep me from throwing the spear at the box, he stood in front of the boxes. (If you are getting ahead of me here, you are right.) I threw the spear, anyway, hitting Theo above his left eyebrow.

If it had been less than an inch lower, it would have gone through his eyeball, into his brain and he would have died. This happened less than a year after we just lost Baby John.

One of Robby's friends saw what had happened and fetched Mama and Fob. Theo was screaming. Blood was flowing swiftly down his pitiful little face. Mama was hysterical, but she was still able to take care of Theo's bleeding . . . but not until she ran into the house and grabbed her Bible with the purple ribbon marking her favorite scripture. She began reading scripture and praying for Theo's healing:

"And when I passed by thee, and saw thee polluted in thine own blood, I said unto thee when thou was in thy blood, LIVE; yea, I said unto thee when thou was in thy blood, LIVE.   (Ezekiel 16:6)
(So much can be said for taking scripture out of context!)

Anyway, while reading that scripture, praying hard, and applying hard pressure to the wounded area, miraculously God healed Theo within minutes, and the bleeding stopped.

Isn't it amazing how praying hard, and applying hard pressure to a wounded area; God will usually heal (stop) the bleeding? Mama found out that this works every time on a nosebleed too! However, she always quoted that scripture for the added success of fast healing.

Meanwhile, back at the box stack, Fob was taking care of me! He always had a switch handy. He began whipping me from head to toe until the switch broke. He yelled, "Brang me anothern!" One of the boys who was watching, grabbed the spear and gave it to Fob and said, "Here, Mr. Waterman, whop'em with this!"

Fob started beating me with the spear. By this time, Mama had Theo's bleeding stopped. She ran out and screamed for Fob to stop beating me, but he was in full rage and just kept laying it on me. With me being only five years old, I couldn't take too much abuse. That spear was mighty strong, and it wasn't about to break. This beating felt endless. I was getting weak and could not beg for mercy any longer. It appears there was some good in our mother because she covered me with her body to stop Fob.

Well, that was the way Fob handled things. If it was a bad situation, the first thing he knew to do would be to start whipping and never ask questions.

So, there you have it: Theo almost got killed, before he was healed. I was beaten, and I was the one who almost died!

Opee related another story that is sure proof of the insanity of our upbringing. Brace yourselves!

Robby, our oldest brother, was only about ten years old, so naturally, he had to do what Fob told him to do. He was out of school that day for some unknown reason. Fob wasn't working on that day, but Mama was. She had a part-time job at a bakery downtown. Fob was at home doing some "spring cleaning," I will call it.

Only a demented, twisted mind would conceive doing this to his children. Fob told Robby to hold me, Opee, and then Theo down. While Robby was holding us down one by one, Fob pulled back the foreskin of our penises. He then proceeded to put a drop of alcohol inside. Talk about burning! I was screaming! Poor Theo was only about three years old. He was screaming and crying so hysterically that he ran into a wall and knocked himself out!

Fob and Robby laughed at us. After Fob had his fun, he told us, "Boys, you see dat chap belt? You tell yor maw 'bout dis, and yor asses will be burnin' badder dan yor dicks!"

Theo was too young to know how to tell Mama. I had been beaten with that damn chap belt plenty of times, so I didn't want that across my naked back if I could avoid it.

Like I said, it took a cruel, sick mind to dream up such a thing to do to a three and a five-year-old child.

Opee tells about the Saturday trips to town.

It was a muggy, hot June day when we all loaded up in the 1929 Model A Ford for a long, boog-a-dy—boog-a-dy slow trip to downtown Mobile for our weekly grocery buying. The seating arrangements were as follows:

- Dad (Fob) - front left driver's seat
- Mom - front right passenger seat, holding Teddy

Back seat:

- Robby - left side by the window,
- Theo - standing in front of him
- Ellen - right side by the window,
- Tooty - standing in front of her
- Opee - (me) squeezed in wherever I could, in that small back seat

It would have been far better for all of us children to have stayed at home. However, with no one to tend to us, so we were forced to make the trek. And a "trek" it would usually be by the end of the day.

About halfway into the trip, Tooty would usually get sick to her stomach. She would start with a whine. One of the boys would say, "Uh-oh!"

Then Tooty would whine louder!

The boys would, "Uh-oh!" louder!

Dad would say, "Whatjew uh-oh'in 'bout?"

"Tooty's gotta go!" one of the boys would say.

Fob would say, "Whatjew mean 'Tooty's gotta go'?"

Now that Tooty had the attention of everyone in the car, she would grab her stomach and let out a loud ghastly growl.

"Tooty, what's wrong wid'jew, girl?"

"I gotta do-do!"

"Gal! Didn't you do dat 'fo we left?"

"Yes, sir."

"And you gotta do it 'gain?"

Fob would now be cussing. He pulled over and told her to get out and do it on the side of the street. She no more than squatted before a floodgate of half-digested lima beans and cornbread were released. Mama somehow came up with a scrap of paper from her purse for her to clean herself with. From then on, we always carried newspapers in case Tooty had another accident in the car. It happened again from time to time.

Sure enough, the next Saturday, we were almost downtown, the same song, second stanza.

Tooty: "Ummmm!"

Boys: "Uh-oh!"

Fob: "What's wrong?"

Boys: "Tooty's gotta go."

Fob: "Well, put down some newspaper."

There was about a square foot of floor space in front of Ellen. The newspapers go down, and Tooty begins to squirt out what looks like a thin gravy.

The sound that accompanies her is the rhythm and sound of a toy machine gun. *Tooot, toot, toot, toooot*, I always thought her name was quite appropriately fitting for her. Anyway, the stench inside that old small car was more than overpowering. By this time, all heads are sticking out of the four windows gasping for fresh air.

Fob: "Dash damn, gal! I'm never gonna take you nowhere with me again!"

Mama: "Fob, the girl has stomach troubles."

It didn't matter to us what she had. It was a terrible inconvenience for all of us to be forced to endure such an ordeal for so long without fresh air. A person does need air to breathe in order to live, you know. We wondered if we might die from asphyxiation. It was hard not being able to breathe from that smell for such a long period of time in that old car. It's a wonder we are still alive today to tell about it.

Once we had made it to our favorite food store, Tooty would have to sit in the car with Fob, because she usually had soiled her clothes. Fob never got out of the car. If it was a hundred degrees in August or thirty degrees in December, he always stayed in the car. Fob always gave Mama a twenty-dollar bill and told her to only spend fifteen of it.

The rest of us kids joyfully went into the food store with Mama to get our weekly allotment of groceries for fifteen dollars. The first aisle we went down was the candy aisle. Mama would get a bag of chocolate peanut clusters. She would place the bag beside her purse, open it, and begin eating the candy. Of course, we were watching her.

We wanted some of those luscious, melt-in-your-mouth, forbidden, heavenly tasting morsels! Mama would look around to make sure no one was looking, and she would slowly give one to each of us when it was safe.

By the time we made it to the last aisle, the bag would be empty. Mama would then hide the empty bag behind some can goods. We were now ready to check out. That was the only time Mama or us children ever got to enjoy candy. There would have been hell to pay if she had bought the candy. That was not allowed!

So, we children learned to steal at a very early age from one of the best, our mama.

We dared not tell Fob about the candy stealing! He would have beaten all of us for sure---- for not saving some for him.

It's one of the Ten Commandments:

"Thou shalt not get caught stealing."

The grocery list was always the same. Mama bought a large box of flour, a large block of lard, many pounds of dried lima beans, a quart of molasses, and occasionally, a chicken.

There was no trunk on a Model-A Ford. Therefore, the groceries had to ride in the back seat with us children. Once we were all packed in, Mama would sit down and hand her purse and sales receipt over to Fob. He would dump the contents of the purse in his lap, count every cent, and make sure the cost and change added up to twenty dollars. He would look it over very closely with his less than first-grade arithmetic skills. He would then give the purse back to Mama and put the bills in his wallet. And the loose change in his change purse. Then finally, he would say, "Gotta save!"

Mama would just sit there, staring straight ahead with her hands folded in her lap, with gritted teeth, and remained silent.

That happened every Saturday. We made a long trek to town, Tooty would get sick, Mama stole the bag of candy, we watched as the purse was emptied and we heard the same old lie that Fob always told. He controlled every penny in the family, and he controlled every person in the family. It was of great consequence to all of us that he also controlled the chap belt on everyone in the family, including our mother.

For clarification, I will describe what a chap belt is. Cowboys wore a pair of durable leather chaps to protect their legs and clothing from the daily wear and tear of riding. A chap belt was used to hold up the pair of chaps. The belt was usually four or more inches wide and went around the rider's waist. Fob did not own a pair of chaps; he did, however, own a chap belt. He thought he looked like a handsome cowboy when wearing it.

Sometimes on the weekends, Fob would dress up like Gene Autrey (who was a famous cowboy back in those days). He wore a white shirt with a white scarf around his neck, blue jeans, his rhinestone belt, and that damn ole chap belt! He would walk up and down the street, singing and playing his guitar. The chap belt boosted his ego and allowed his fantasies to run rampant. He envisioned himself as a handsome, tough, courageous, and desirable man. Truth is, he was a nasty, crude, and violent worm of a man. When he would return home, the demon would return with him, the same ole Fob as before, mean as hell!

When he wasn't wearing that damn ole chap belt, it was used as a beating device. No one outside of the family ever knew, just us, and none of us were talking.

Can you imagine beating a child with a four-inch, hard leather weapon? I don't have to; it happened to me regularly from age four to fifteen years old. Most of the time, I never knew why.

Rob proudly wearing his chap belt.

4.
More Nursery Rhymes

Question: "Why did the children cross the road?"
Answer: "To get away from the hell hole!"

Letters and memories from Opee

Robby, Ellen, and I walked about a mile to school. Robby was in seventh grade; Ellen was in fifth. I was in second. I felt sorry for Ellen. All we had to make for lunch was potted meat spread on a biscuit. Here's how to make it: Break open the biscuit, spread the meat, wrap it in a piece of newspaper, and carry it in your pocket. Poor Ellen! After a breakfast of cold syrup, cold biscuit, and water, she would be hungry before she got to school, but she was ashamed to eat a biscuit in the lunchroom. She would give her biscuit to Robby or me. Then she would go all day with nothing to eat. Later in the evening, we would have lima beans, cornbread, and water for supper.

I don't know if there was anything that Mama could have done to provide us with a decent lunch at school. But that was our life, and we didn't complain. I didn't care for the potted meat biscuits, but it beat not having anything. And believe me! Watching those lucky kids eating a hot meal in the lunchroom made that potted meat biscuit taste even the more worse! (If that could possibly be so.)

I believe the first one at fault on those bad times was the sorry bastard Fob. Mama wasn't far behind. That money-grubbing Fob had us on a starvation diet because he only let Mama buy certain foods.

The same damn thing every week. "Gotta save money," he would always say.

Here is another quote from the *Great One*: "Waste not, want not." Fob always said that quote because he never threw anything away. Here's an example. If we had a pot that got a small hole it in, Fob would get out his little "mend-it kit." He would put a screw in the bottom of the pot and then a nut to hold the screw in place. That sealed the hole in the pot and saved him a dollar from having to buy another pot. *Voila!* Brilliance in action!

Poor ignorant Fob! He thought he was quoting scripture when he said, "Waste not, want not." He had no idea where that proverbial phrase came from.

John Wesley first recorded "He will waste nothing; but he must want nothing," in 1772.

An even earlier version; "willful waste makes woeful want" was recorded in 1721.

Well, at least Fob knew how to make a good application to that idiom's meaning, even if he didn't know it wasn't in the Bible.

Mama did her share of making our young lives miserable with her beatings. She could swing a switch or belt just as hard as Fob could! She seemed to enjoy it too! Hell! The woman got beatings herself while growing up as a child. She knew how painful they were. She hollered and begged her dad, grandpappy, to stop beating her, just as we did. Our begging never stopped the whippings. We received no pity from either of our so-called parents. Mama received abuse as a child, and she grew up to be a victimizer. What a shame! It didn't have to be that way.

To this day, I believe Mama was only half-sane at any given time. She was a walking, talking, ticking, time bomb. It is crazy how the whole family revolves around the mama, and when that mama is half crazy, it makes the whole family half crazy! It is no wonder she was only half sane, with a house full of children wanting or needing something from her all day! There were cooking and laundry to be done; sometimes field work, then almost every night there was tending to Fob's physical needs in bed. We could hear that chap belt bouncing against the wall, hanging by a nail, as the bed would jar the wall. We all knew what was going on.

Mama didn't like it. I believe she hated Fob. She knew she was stuck with the sorry bastard. That is probably why she had so much rage built up. She couldn't take it out on him, so there we were. It's a damn shame that she treated us as badly as she did. Our life with Fob was bad enough by itself. She only made it worse. We didn't have one parent to protect us from the other! So, we got a double dose!

Another story from Opee

I mentioned Mama doing the laundry. We all did the laundry. All four of the children and Mama got together with four, number 2 wash tubs and scrubbed the clothes on a rubboard using a box of Octagon soap. The first tub was used to scrub the clothes, then ring out some of the cold water. The second tub was used as a quick rinse. The third tub was used as a second rinse. The fourth tub was used to carry the wet, soaking clothes to the clothesline and hang them out to dry. It sometimes took days for them to dry because they were so soaked. Needless to say, our clothing always smelled foul because of the Octagon soap and then the sour smell because it took so long to dry. Sometimes, the clothes got another rinse if it rained.

We thought we were rich when we didn't have to scrub the clothes anymore on that rubboard. After years of begging, Fob broke down and bought Mama a wringer-type washing machine. We still had to run them through the wringer, then hang them out to dry, but it sure was a lot less work.

One day, Tooty was playing with the wringer. The two wringer rollers had a lot of pressure on them. She got her hand caught by the rollers. She screamed. Ellen saw what was happening and struck the release bar. It was lucky for Tooty! If Ellen had not been there, the rollers would have torn Tooty's little frail hand apart! Tooty escaped with bruises and a squashed little hand. Those pains were nothing compared to the whipping she got when Fob came home. The stupid bastard thought she had broken the new washing machine, which she had not. She was just a kid looking for something fun to play with. After all, she had no toys, and the new washing machine was new and interesting. Shame on Fob, mostly for being so stupid!

Opee tells about the game of bump-bump

It was in early June of 1951. Mama was just a few weeks away from delivering Ana. She and I were working in the vegetable garden. Theo and Tooty were somewhere else playing. Theo was around eight and a half years old, and Tooty was four and a half.

Tooty came running up to Mama and said, "Me and Theo done learnt to play a new game called bump-bump."

Mama asked, "<u>Really</u>, how do you play this new game?"

Tooty said, "We pull down our pants, Theo puts his thang up to my thang, and we say bump-bump."

I noticed Theo standing about fifty feet away. He was watching out of the corner of his eye. Mama screamed, "Theo! Get over here!"

Theo started crying. When Mama told him what Tooty had told her, he tried to beg off. It did no good! "When yor daddy gets home, he's gonna whop you!" Mama said. That statement terrified Theo, poor boy! He really started to beg then!

"Mama, please, don't tell Daddy! Don't let Daddy whop me!"

Begging wasn't helping him. He went into the house and came back with the chap belt and begged Mama to whip him with it. She wouldn't.

I believe she was too far into the pregnancy to expend the energy necessary to really inflict the pain on Theo that she thought he deserved.

Poor Tooty, she just stood there and never said another word. She just had a blank look on her face. Being only four and a half years old, she had no idea what she was talking about.

After crying and begging for about an hour, we heard that damn dinner bell ring! That brought a new and heightened fear into Theo! He let out a high screech of terror, as he ran and hid.

Robby and Fob walked into the front yard, Mama went out and met them. She told Fob what Tooty had told her. Fob became a raging maniac! He started screaming at Theo, "Com-mere, boy! Gim-me dat chap belt! Yor gonna get a whoppin'!"

Theo's crying turned into a higher pitched squeal. It sounded like a woman screaming. Now, keep in mind, the only clothes that Theo had on was a pair of short pants. He only weighed about sixty pounds, skin, and bones.

Fob dragged Theo into the middle room of the streetcar/house. Between the two rooms of the house, there were boards nailed over the windows with one-inch cracks between them. When one of us was getting a whipping/beating, the others would peek through the cracks, being very thankful that it wasn't happening to us.

Mama was sitting at the table with Tooty. Robby, Ellen, and I were peeking through the cracks. We didn't peek too long. It was so bad; we couldn't bear to see what was happening to our brother. Fob was hitting his little skinny body so hard with that heavy chap belt, that Theo's body was bouncing up and down off the mattress; flipping over and getting hit everywhere all over his frail body. At one point the chap belt landed on Theo's crotch. Our poor little brother let out an even wilder tormented howl, grabbing and holding himself in that area for protection.

With no mercy, Fob said, "You better hold on to 'dem cods, boy!"

I expected and wanted Mama to stop the beating. She didn't.

After Fob had vented his rage, he finally ceased the torture. He dragged Theo to the table and said, "Sit down!"

We were horrified at the belt marks on Theo. Blue, green, red, and turning black! His little muscles were flitting out of control. We could see the ripples under his skin jerking and twitching. It would have taken a lot of crying to help get over the pain that Theo was experiencing. But it wasn't to be.

Fob yelled at Theo, "Boy, that damn cryin' stops rat now! Yore gonna eat this meal and shut up or yor gonna get some more chap belt. You want some more chap belt?"

Theo managed to mumble, "Noooooo, sir."

I don't know how Theo managed to eat those damn big lima beans, cornbread, and water that night without choking to death. Had he strangled to death or needed medical attention; Fob would have had to explain why he beat that small, frail, skinny child so severely.

He was worthless.

Opee was eleven years old and remembers when Ana was born.

In the summer of 1951, our baby sister was born, Ana. A bouncing seven-pound bundle of energy. Within a few months, she could walk, and it was hard to keep up with her. Teddy did an excellent job of it, however. Soon they were both all about the flower nursery grounds. We don't know who got whom into the trouble, but they sure got into it! The two were always into exploring things. Mama had a hard time keeping up with them. She was so busy with her chores, it's a wonder that she knew how many children she had at any one time. The only time the two would come home was when there was an emergency. Like the time Ana stuck a field pea up her nose. Mama had to dig it out with Ana blowing her nose and crying. It was great entertainment for all of us to watch. Nothing exciting or funny ever happened around our house, but this was funny!

In the fall of 1951, our oldest brother Robby met a new friend at the fillin' station that was on the highway and around the corner from our streetcar/house. My brother Robby was good at making friends. He liked to play his guitar and sing, and he was good at it. One day, he brought home a guy named Fred, who was the ugliest and stinkiest man that we had ever met. He was even nastier than we were! He seemed to be a likable guy anyway. We never had anyone to talk to, other than the nine of us, so most anyone new was a welcomed change. Robby and Fred would play their guitars and sing. This was a fresh change of entertainment for all of us. Fred came around reasonably often. It wasn't long before Fred took a liking to Mama, or was it the other way around? Fred came around more and more often to visit and play guitars with Robbie. It wasn't long before we thought of Fred as family. Little did we know how soon he would be family.

Before Fred took a liking to Mama, he fell in heat for our oldest sister, Ellen. Ellen and Skeeter were sweethearts at the time and had just started talking about marriage.

One Sunday morning, Robby, Fred, and Skeeter were hunting around the nursery grounds for rabbits. Skeeter was walking ahead of Robbie and Fred. Fred leaned over and whispered to Robbie, "If you'll shoot Skeeter in the back, he'll be dead, and I'll have a chance with Ellen. I'll lie and say I saw you stumble, and the shooting was an accident." Robbie responded, "You crazy son-of-a-bitch! I'm not going to murder Skeeter for you to get to Ellen! If you want him dead, you shoot him!"

If either of them had killed Skeeter, they probably could have lied and gotten away with it. However, there was no way in hell that Ellen was so desperate that she would take up with a worm such as Fred!

Poor ugly, filthy Fred! He wanted the beautiful young daughter and got stuck with the old-worn-out Mama!

In the summer of 1952, I, Opee, was eleven years old. Fob still worked at the Little Wild Wood Flower Nursery. He asked the owners if they might give me a job pulling grass and weeds. The owners asked how old I was. Fob lied and said that I was twelve. For some reason, it mattered that I should be twelve years old. The workdays were Monday through Friday, 6:30 a.m. until 12:00 noon. Then 1:00 p.m. until 4:30 p.m. On Saturday, 6:30 a.m. until 11:30 a.m. I was paid $12.50 a week for all those hours. There was never a mention of how much of the $12.50 that I would be able to keep. That was something that we all knew better than to ask for—money!

After the first week, at 11:30, the bell rang. We all went to the office, and the secretary gave each of us a small brown pay envelope. I was so excited to receive my very first pay for my hard-earned work in the scorching sun. As Fob and I walked the short distance back to the streetcar, that we called our home, he whispered, "Don't you open dat up. Don't give it to me while they are looking. Wait 'til we get home, then give it to me."

Keep in mind, I wasn't expecting anything. But I was hoping to get some money for all those hours of hot, sweaty, hard labor. Fob opened my envelope. He took out the cash: a ten, two ones, and a fifty-cent piece. I detected an almost imperceptible look on his face as he fondled the coin, then he handed it to me. He then turned and went into the house. I was elated! Happy! Joyful! Giddy! This was the first time I actually had money in my dirty, tired, sweaty hands ... and I could spend it all on me!

For the rest of that week, I went to work every day imagining what I would spend my fifty cents on the following Saturday.

The second Saturday, the same thing happened. The bell rang, I received my little brown envelope, walked back to the house with Fob, and I handled my hard-earned money over to him. He again saw the cash—one ten, two ones, and a fifty-cent piece.

The slightly strange look on his face wasn't there that day, as he opened my envelope. The son-of-a-bitch had made up his mind that if there was another fifty-cent piece in the envelope, he would keep it! He took out his change purse, took out a quarter, handed it to me, and walked into the house without a word!

Talk about a letdown! I practically dreamed about that fifty-cent piece all week! I went into some bushes across the dirt road, hid and cried like a baby. I grew up some that day. I didn't realize it at that time, but it was then and there that I learned not to be an optimist.

The next year, the nursery owners allowed Theo to work there. The cheap bastards only paid him twenty cents an hour. I guess it didn't matter what we got paid at the old nursery, the only thing we got paid from Fob was a lousy quarter.

In memory of Robby:

In January of 1953, Robby was seventeen when he enlisted with the Marines and left our hellhole of a place, we called home. A few years earlier, Fob forced him to quit school after seventh grade. He continued to work at the nursery and give all his money to Mama. Robby knew there was more to life than what he was experiencing. Fob was mad as hell and demanded that he stay and work with him. I guess Fob had hopes that Robby would stay and continue to give him the money he was earning. Robby was smarter than that. He was tall, very handsome, and we all thought of him as the most intelligent of the siblings. At the time, Robby was the smartest because he was the oldest. Robby had been a good son, and a loyal son at that; but he had endured all the physical and mental abuse he was willing to accept. That day in 1953, Robby left us to make a life of his own in the United States Marine Corps. As a matter of fact, he made a career of it. Robby came home occasionally to visit and bring us gifts from various places all over the world, where he had been. On one of his visits home, he met a pretty little blonde, fell in love, and eventually they married. Together they had two beautiful children. While in the Marines, Robby's pride were his hundreds (and I do mean hundreds) of medals and awards for Top Marksmanship of various weaponry. Many awards were national honors. Robby stayed in the Marines until he retired as Captain. He then lived a peaceful life in South Carolina until his death at the age of seventy-three. We all loved him; he was a good big brother.

Theo and Opee working at the nursery.

Opee shares another nursery rhyme

It was a freezing day in December. The temperature was in the thirties, and ice was sticking up out of the ground. It was overcast, and the wind was blowing fiercely. That money-loving piece of crap, Fob took Theo and me to work with him. We only made $ 0.25 and $ 0.20 an hour to pull grass. Well, grass doesn't grow in the winter! But Fob wanted every penny he could get his hands on. We went to work that morning wearing only pants, shirts, and a windbreaker. That was all we had to keep us warm. By the time we got to the barn, we were freezing. Mr. Swatty, our boss, should have sent us back home because there was no grass to pull. Instead, he took us to a lathe house and pointed to the potted plants and said, "start pulling." Our hands were so cold they hurt. I gathered up some pine straw and put it in a gallon can and lit it. As we were warming our hands, Mr. Swatty came up and demanded that we put out the fire. He was worried that we might set the lathe house on fire. What he said and what he meant were two different things. What he meant was, "if you boys spend all morning warming your hands, you won't be able to pull grass."

We said, "yes, sir," and put out the fire. In about ten minutes, our hands were really hurting. I started another fire. Mr. Swatty came to us again and said, "I told you boys, to put out that fire. Now put it out or go home."

I put out the fire, and in about ten more minutes, Theo and I were suffering damn near frostbite. I told Theo that we couldn't stay out in that weather any longer, so we went home. Theo wanted to go home and sit by the old pot-belly stove as much as I did. We knew it would be one more whipping from Fob if he found out. I said, "Let's go." We were willing to risk the beating anyway! As soon as we walked through the door, Mama wanted to know, "What's wrong?" I told her. She said, "You know what yor daddy's gonna do ta ya!" Yes, we knew, but we were freezing.

We got to work that morning at 6:30 a.m., and we were back home by 7:30 a.m. The bell rang at 11:30 a.m. Hell was on the way home! Fob came storming through the door! Cursing and saying that the Swatty's didn't want Theo and me to work for them anymore. Mama headed off our beatings by taking our sides. She told Fob that he had no business putting us young'uns out in that freezing weather like that! Fob knew he was wrong. I believe that was the only reason that he didn't whip us that day. I sure was dreading that whipping that I was for sure was about to happen to us.

That money-grubbing bastard, Fob, wanted the $2.25 that Theo and I *would have made that day* had we work the full hours. He didn't give a damn what Theo and I had to suffer through to get it.

It was about a week or two later that we heard Fob had quit his job at the Little Wild Wood Flower Nursery and we were moving. A few days after that, we learned the truth. Fob had tried to get the Swatty's to take Theo and I back on as workers, and they wouldn't. They had an argument, and Fob got fired. I am glad that I put mine and Theo's little boney asses at risk that day. Otherwise, there is no telling how much longer we would have had to stay, live, and work in that *hellhole* of a place called the Little Wild Wood Flower Nursery!

5.
Existing on Moffia Road

Some of the events that happened to me in this chapter; I remember. Other events that happened to my siblings were told to me by my brother, Opee; of which I do not remember. The reader will be able to distinguish the difference.

It was the latter part of December 1953, and the winter was frigid that year. We were getting packed up to move away from the flower nursery. We were moving to our new home on Forrester Street, just off Moffia Road. The house wasn't a new house, just another house. We were all glad that it wasn't a streetcar, with an addition built on to it, like the one we were living in at the nursery. This other house was an actual shotgun house, with three rooms consecutive one after another. Front bedroom, middle bedroom, and a back kitchen. Soon after we moved there, Fob built a tiny lean-to room that attached to the kitchen. That was where Theo and I, (Opee), slept together on a roll-away bed. The room was barely large enough for the bed; however, it did serve as an extra bedroom at the time, and we were glad to have it. The middle room is where the pot-belly stove was located. This is where the family huddled around to keep warm. We also had a front and back porch. The outhouse was located to the lower left rear corner of the yard, within smelling distance.

A storm drainage ditch ran along the side of the old unpainted shack. We thought it was a creek. As a matter of fact, we called it a creek. Sometimes, during heavy floods, the creek would rise. I can still see Fob standing on that rickety unpainted back porch with a broomstick in his hand, testing to see how deep the creek had risen. I was afraid that if I had fallen into the water, I would be washed away forever. It's a good thing it never happened; otherwise, I would not be here today to write this story!

Our next-door neighbors on Forrester Street were actually worse off than we were. There were at least three children in the family that I can remember: Jakie, Toola, and Poo-Dink Forrester. I guess the street must have been named after them. We believe they were a Cajun family, and like us, they were also white trash. They lived on welfare. No one in their family worked. They cooked their meals on a wood-burning stove, which was also used to keep them warm. No one ever saw their mama go outside of the house. They were a pitiful family. Even we felt sorry for them! That's about all I have to say about them. Except this: Years later, Opee worked at a drugstore, and he made a delivery to one of the Forrester girl's homes. She was an adult with a sick baby. She was still living on welfare.

> *The event that I am about to share is indeed grotesque. I am totally embarrassed to write these words on paper. However, I must let it be known to the world how repulsive, repugnant, and obnoxious this man called Fob truly was. And we had to call him Daddy.*

In the words of Opee:

Fob was a crude bastard. He rarely got an all-over-body-bath in a washtub. For sleeping, he wore boxer shorts and a ribbed T-shirt. Every night, the same thing would happen. The old battery-powered radio would be going; Mama would be lying in one bed, and Fob would be lying in the other. We children would sit on the floor around Fob's bed to hear the radio better.

We all watched as Fob was lying on his back. He would run his hand down the front of his boxers, scratch his ass, and bring out his brown-stained "fangers," then sniff them. His nostrils would flare, and he would make snorting sounds. We pretended not to see; Mama just ignored him.

Fob thought it was a funny game. It was another night, with the same setup. The usual stinky Fob in his bed, and the same little innocent victims. When I say victims, I mean kids sitting on the floor close enough to be grabbed.

I saw Fob's right-hand dive into his boxers. I thought *It's just another disgusting display of ass scratching and sniffin'.* This time it was different. Fob had the insane idea that he thought it would be funny if the right hand came out of his boxers with brown-stained "fangers" and he grabbed the nearest child to him. At that time, it was Theo. He grabbed Theo by the hair, pulled his head back, and thrust his hand into Theo's nose and said, "Boy, smell my fangers!"

Theo was hard to hold. He started screaming, "Mama, Daddy's makin' me smell his 'fangers'! I'mma gonna puke!"

Fob yelled, "Boy! Don't you puke on dat floor!"

Mama responded, "Fob, stop doin' dat ta Theo! You gonna make him puke!"

Theo was struggling for clean air. Some of the brown stuff was under and on top of his nose. He slid away and out of Fob's distance, still crying and whimpering. Theo only looked back once at Fob with hatred in his eyes. Mama got out of bed and cleaned Theo's face.

I'll tell you this, after that night, we all still sat around on the floor listening to the radio shows, and we had to sit close to Fob's bed in order to hear. But when his hand took a dive into his boxers, we all looked like a covey of cockroaches, scooting across the floor, away from Fob!

He'd be left by himself, sniffing like a hungry buzzard on a rotten pile of roadkill.

For the life of me, I do not know what good Fob got out of that sickening exhibition!

Ana remembers when Mary came home right after her birth.

It was January 1954, when I, Ana, was told that Mama was away at the hospital and would soon be home with my baby sister. At that time, I was the baby, and I loved it. But now there would be one younger than me, my baby sister! Now, I would have a baby doll of my very own to play with and take care of.

I anxiously waited and watched out the front window of our unpainted, dilapidated shotgun house for the 1939 black Ford to pull up. Finally, there it came clunking down the red dirt hill. In it was Fob, Mama, and a little bundle of blob that I could hardly make out what in the world it was. The old black car slowly rolled to a stop, then it let out a backfire as if to say, "There . . . I quit!"

The passenger side door opened as I was running up to meet the new arrival. There was Mama holding something all bundled up in a blanket with no head to be seen. It could have been a cat as far as I could tell.

I said, "Is that my baby sister?"

Mama said, "Yes."

I said, "Give her to me," as I stretched out my arms.

"You can't have her yet," Mama said.

I was disappointed when I was not given my baby sister, which I was told would be my baby sister. I cried because I couldn't hold her at first. I was okay after I learned that I had to sit down to hold her. She was pretty;

I thought she looked like a little angel baby—my angel baby.

As a little time passed, we noticed that our newest little angel baby sister didn't look like the rest of us. Her hair had more of a strawberry-blonde tint to it. Her eyes seemed to be more green than blue, as were ours. Mama tried to convince Fob that she looked like Opee. Fob, being so stupid, would just shake his head in agreement. No one really noticed who the new baby really looked like, except Mama. Mama had a secret; we would later learn what the mystery was, as to who our new baby sister actually resembled.

My baby sister's name was Mary. I loved her with all my heart, and I looked out for her and cared for her until the day she died at the age of fifty-two.

Mary was the kindest, most gentle lady that I have ever known. Not one unkind word did I ever hear come from her sweet little mouth. Being such a humble person, she would get taken advantage of sometimes, but not if I was around!

I love you, Mary; I will see you again in heaven . . . my dear "Sissy."

More hellish stories from Ana

From time to time, Mama would take the bus to downtown. I don't know why she had to take care of business in town, but she would usually leave while Fob was at work. At that time, Fob had a job driving a dump truck, hauling dirt. He had no idea that she would leave. When Mama was gone, the children were left to their own devices. Most of the time, we were up to no good. When Mama returned from her mystery trip, I would tattle-tell on the older kids for whatever they had done naughty. Most of the time, it was talking about "bumping." I knew that was wrong.

Being the smallest left behind and tattle-telling when Mama returned was not a good thing to do, I learned very quickly.

The time Mama went to town, my brother, Theo, would sit on my head with a pillow, as revenge because I had tattled on him the prior time. I mean, he would sit on my head for a very long time. I would kick and scream, gasping for air. I thought I was going to die. I probably damn near did die a few times. Theo thought it was funny. I did not! I never liked Theo for doing that to me, nor did I ever forget about it.

You see, Theo was a *victim* of child abuse, and he was learning at his very young age to be a *victimizer*. How could he not? He was learning it from the best . . . Fob!

I realize that poverty is a cesspool that can breed uncivilized behavior, but it cannot be excused. I knew children who were just as poor as we, but they were clean and well mannered. I believe there is something to be said for the old Southern expression: "Poor but proud." The crude actions of the children lay squarely on the parents!

We all make decisions in our lives. You may be a victim, but you don't have to be a victimizer. You can choose to overcome all of that and be a victor! The decision is yours.

The next few times, Mama would get ready to leave, I would beg her to take me with her. I was afraid that Theo was going to sit on my head with a pillow and kill me. I was only four years old and not big enough to defend myself. I was glad when she started taking me with her. I found out what the great mystery was all about. She was meeting Fred.

Unbeknownst to all of us, Mama and Fred had been having an affair since the fall of 1951. That was right after

I was born. Mary was born in 1954, she was Fred's child. I didn't think anything of Mama and Fred meeting with one another; Fred was our family friend. So, during these friendly visits, Mary and I usually laid in the back seat of Fred's car, played and napped while Mama and Fred talked and smooched and screwed…I guess…. hell, I know they did!

One day, after returning home from a hot afternoon of Mama smooching with Fred, Fob said to me, "Baby girl, let's you and me go fer a little walk."

He asked me where we had been. He said, "I'll buy ya some ice creamie if ya tell me whar ya been wif ya Maw."

Of course, I wanted that yummy ice cream, so I sold out my mama. I told him that we went riding with Fred. Fob was furious! He bought me that nickel ice cream then hurried back to the house and started shouting at mama. He lit into her unmercifully! Mama was screaming that she didn't know what he was talking about, but he just kept on slapping her. I felt terrible about having told on Mama. All for a nickel ice cream. That day we learned another one of those commandments.

"Thou shalt not admit adultery."

Opee was fourteen years old in 1954 when he recalls this:

Although Mama and all her brothers and sisters were brought up in the same type of family environment where their daddy beat them also; Mama's other siblings married well and moved on to make a good life for themselves. They were good decent people. Not Mama. She had the bad luck of having to marry her first cousin at the age of fifteen and get stuck in a horrible situation.

I know that Mama's brothers and sisters would have liked to help her and us, but what could they do? They had their own families to take care of. Can you imagine the hell one of them would have caught from Fob if we had been allowed to go and live with one of them?

I can't blame them for looking the other way. Dumbass Fob had no idea that his in-laws, who were actually his cousins, despised him! They only tolerated him because they wanted to see Mama.

I will never forget how embarrassed Mama would get on the rare times that Fob would take us to visit one of them. Fob would park in the front yard and start blowing the car horn. We weren't allowed to open a door until an adult family member would come out and welcome us in. I can't tell you how many times Mama would beg him to not blow the horn.

Fob would say, "If they wanna see us, they'll come out."

If they didn't come out within a short time, we would leave. Most of the time, someone always came out.

On the infrequent times that they came to visit us, they would pull up into the yard, and walk up to our door.

While we children loved to visit with our cousins, we were always under the evil-eye-watch of Fob. He'd always tell us before we got there, "You young'uns better behave and mind-out now; I'll be watchin' ya. If I have to 'cut my eye' at ya, you'll get a good whoppin' when we get home."

To ourselves, we would groan. I mean, who in the hell can have fun playing with the other children when Fob was leering and hoping for some reason to whip one of us? He didn't want to be there visiting, anyway. So, he would make the trip worth his while…. when he got home, he would take his anger out on one of us.

It would usually be Theo or me to get the "cut my eye at ya." When it was me that got his evil eye, I would be hit with an instant freeze. I would feel cold all over, it made me sick and shakey, and I would have to go sit down. I knew I was going to get beaten as soon as we got home. Most of the time, I would have no idea what I had done wrong. I probably did nothing wrong. The sorry S.O.B. would just make up something "wrong" that we had done. He would never tell you what you had done wrong. We would beg on the way home, "Daddy, what did I do?"

Fob would say, "Boy, don't ask me wot you did. You knowed wot you wuz a doin' when I 'cut my eye' at ya!"

There was no appeal. Mama just kept her mouth shut.

Well, I got that whipping when we got home. It wasn't as bad as some that I had received in the past, so I didn't cry. I just laid there on the bed and took it. I thought I was tough by not crying. After all, I was now fourteen years old. That was a big mistake! This didn't sit well with Fob. To Fob, part of the joy of beating the children was watching them being debased and demoralized.

About a week later, I was out in the front yard. Theo came out whimpering, looking for me. He said, "Daddy's goin' whop you. He done whop me, and yor next."

Now, here I am, the eternal optimist, thinking, *Yeah! So, he's going to whip me again! He whipped me last week, and I took it. I'll take this one too.*

I found out back then that every time I tried to be optimistic about anything, I usually lost, and now I'm about to lose again---big time! It happened this way:

The middle room had the wood burning heater set up. All the family was huddled around it to keep warm because it was approximately thirty degrees outside. There was a bed in front of the heater. As soon as I walked into the room, Fob slammed me down on the bed and grabbed up a short piece of one-inch-by-four-inch board that was used as firewood.

Fob started yelling, "Boy, when I whopped you last week, you didn't cry. Well, you gonna cry tonight!" At that time, he sat down on my back and started swinging that piece of one-inch-by-four-inch on my skinny ass. His weight was crushing the air out of my lungs. But he wanted me to cry, so I cried as loud as I could with what little air that I could get out.

He was hitting me so hard with the board that he was knocking the feeling out of me, I didn't feel the blows. (I am sure there must be a medical term for that.) He must have hit me fifteen or more times.

When he got off me, he yanked me up to my feet and started slapping my face on both sides. He was yelling something, but I had no idea what he was saying. He then told Theo and me to go to bed. Mama did not say anything.

Theo and I shared the same five-feet-by-six-feet roll-a-way bed that was in the back room, off from the kitchen.

I took off my clothes and sat on the bed. About that time, the feeling came back into my butt. It felt like someone had stuck a knife in my butt cheeks! I jumped off the bed. Theo said, "What's wrong?" I pulled down my shorts and what I saw scared me; it scared Theo too! My ass was all the colors of the rainbow, plus black. It was then that I saw the damage that one-inch-by-four-inch board, used as a weapon, had done to me. The rest of my butt had regained its feeling, and all the pain set in. So, what I didn't feel during the beating, I was making up for now.

I didn't get any sleep that night. I wanted to cry, but I knew better. I never told Mama or Fob about the damage that was done to my black and blue ass and legs.

Another week passed. It was on a Saturday night in 1955, and Fob for some unknown reason was going to lay it on me again. I was still recovering from my previous injuries. I knew I couldn't survive another beating on top of the last one.

I got lucky. Mama gave me a $1 bill and told me to go to the store across the road and pay a bill.

All I had on was tennis shoes, blue jeans, a shirt, and a windbreaker jacket. The temperature was going down into the twenties that night. As soon as I got to Moffia Road, I stuck out my thumb. The first car that came by picked me up. Where I was going? I had no idea. But anywhere was better as long as it was away from Mama and Fob and that beating that he was going to give me later that night.

That first car took me a little way down the road to the next town of Wilsonville. I stuck out my thumb again. Another car picked me up. This car took me to a little town in Mississippi called Lucyville. It was rapidly approaching dark. There was a flower nursery near the road. I knew about working at a flower nursery, so I walked up and asked the owner for a job. He asked my age. I told him I was fourteen. He said, "Boy, you need to be in school and not looking for work."

Disheartened, I found a movie theater. The movie playing was *Frances the Talking Mule*. I used up most of that dollar bill on the ticket, popcorn, and a small coke. I sat through the movie a couple of times, to get my money's worth.

Well, here I go again. Back on the highway with my thumb out hitchhiking. A guy driving a freight truck picked me up. It was about midnight. He wanted to know where I was going. I told him I was running away from home. He wanted to know "why?" After I told him my long sad story, he began talking some sense into me. He told me what a big mistake I was making. I was a boy of only fourteen years old with no money. He told me that I was headed for a lot more pain and misery on the road than the ass whipping that was waiting for me when I returned home.

He made his delivery that night and then told me that if I took his advice, he would drop me off at our house. I took him up on his offer and his excellent advice. That good man probably saved my life that night. I was too young to get a job. I probably would have turned to a life of crime to get by in life.

I sure hated to knock on that front door of our house at 2:00 a.m. that morning! Fob and Mama had been awake all night, waiting for that knock. If I had returned after only a few hours, I am sure the ass beating would have commenced. But after ten hours of being gone, they were pretty sure I had run away. They seemed angry that I had left but certainly not worried.

They asked where I had been. I lied and told them I had been at a boy's house up the road watching television. They both knew I was lying, but all they said was, "Go to bed." I wanted them to care that I had run away, but they didn't. I was glad I didn't get that beating!

I crawled into bed next to Theo. He told me when it appeared that I was not coming back home, Fob started blaming Mama for causing me to run away.

The next morning, Fob took Theo and me to a local sawmill to get free short pieces of lumber to burn in the heater. Looking at those short pieces of one-inch-by-four-inch boards, reminded me that my ass was blistered with a board just like those the day previously.

There was an old man there, also getting a load of the free wood for his heater. Fob told the old man, "My boy here (pointing to me) is the only one of my young'uns to run away from home. He left us last night, but he got hungry and came back home to his pa."

I was so damn glad not to have my already battered ass blistered again that I could have danced and sang! That last beating was the last one that I ever got. It was one hell of a going-away present! One that I will never forget!

I, Ana, was only four when I got my last whipping from Fob.

A few years back, Fob started buying penicillin. If one of the children coughed or sniffled, he would grab the one almost rusty, dull needle and fill the syringe with penicillin. He would tell one of the bigger children, "Hold that gal (or boy) . . ." Then he or she would get the shot. The shots hurt and burned! Being kids, we'd kick and scream at the sight of that big dull needle and the bottle of medicine. Sometimes, kicking the bottle out of Fob's hands before he could stick the needle in us. This only made matters worse. Then, we would not only get that horrible injection of penicillin but a whipping to follow!

It was to be my last whipping from Fob, all because he wanted to give me a shot. It was 1955, I was four years old. My brother Teddy and I were the next *victims* on the receiving end of that old dull needle! Teddy and I were lying across the bed on our stomachs. I was screaming and kicking, trying to escape. Teddy said, "Jus' grit ya teeth and bear it!" Easy for him to say--he was a boy! ---And a year older at that. Teddy took his shot like a man, was done and gone. I continued to be a sissy baby, crying uncontrollably, trying to escape.

Mama was the unlucky one who had to do the holding. With my uncontrollable kicking, the whipping started. First, Mama tried to get between Fob and me. She was willing to take the whipping for me, and she did. After Fob whipped Mama, I then got the penicillin shot anyway.

It's a wonder we all didn't get some sort of infection from that nasty, blunt needle that he reused over and over.

After Fob beat Mama, she went to the kitchen and proceeded to make our dinner. Her hands were in the biscuit bowl and full of wet dough. Fob came in to continue the fight. He slapped Mama, and her glasses nearly fell off. Well, that was all it took! Mama handed her glasses to one of the older kids and said, "Hold'em." Then she threw a hand full of biscuit dough onto Fob's face. All hell broke loose! Fob was slapping, slinging, and choking Mama. He was slamming her head up against the wall. They were both screaming and cussing at one another as the blows were being passed. Needless to say, Fob won. Mama was a bloody mess and hurt badly.

Mama hobbled into the middle bedroom, where the shots all started. She was sitting on the side of the bed, crying. I came in and put my arm around her shoulder to console her. After all, it was my fault that she got the beating. I was standing next to her, loving on her when Fob entered the room. I guess he was making some sort of attempt to make up with her. Mama immediately rejected him by pushing him away. In defiance to Mama, he laughed, turned around, put his big fat butt in her face, and farted!

Fob, that was the man we called "Dad"...
What a hellhound!

I was glad to hear later in my life that "Soldier Boy" was my real father, whoever he was.

We were told that Mama made trips to town as a way to escape from Fob. On one of those trips, she met a good-looking soldier and started talking. The conversation ended in a hotel room. It was only one occasion, and I was conceived. Mama told this story more than once.

Thank you, Soldier Boy, you must have been handsome, smart, and talented.

6.
She Left Us Before She Was Gone

It was late spring of 1955. The school was almost out, and the older children were looking forward to warmer summer days. The winter had been quite cold in that drafty, rundown, shotgun house. Now the birds were singing, and the trees were budding out.

All seemed well for us on that day---until Mama started packing her little worn-out, cardboard suitcase and putting everything she owned into it. Also, in that tattered suitcase were mine and Mary's clothes, what sparingly little we both had.

Opee, Theo, and Tooty stood watching her in disbelief! Mama had suffered the brutal beatings from Fob all she was willing to take. Now she had finally gotten up the nerve to leave him. That would have been a good thing, except she was leaving her children too.

Theo just stood there, pitiful. He never showed any feelings, remorse, love, or guilt, ever in his life. Today was no different. He only had an empty, blank stare on his face when he would occasionally look up at Mama, watching her pack. Other than that, he just looked down at his dirty, crusty bare feet, and occasionally, shuffled on them.

Opee, being the oldest child still at home, was trying to act mature and understanding. He tried to appeal to Mama only once by saying, "Mama, don't leave." However, knowing that Mama was a violent person, he dared not to push her too far for fear of her full-face slap, which came swiftly and unexpected when she was riled.

Tooty, being only eight years old, was not so restrained. Whining and crying uncontrollably, she said, "Mama, don't leave me! Mama, don't leave me!" Tooty was fidgeting and twisting her hair into tangles, then she grabbed at Mama's skirt tail in a hopeless attempt at getting Mama to stay. Mama glared down at her, said nothing, and kept on with her mission.

Teddy and I were staying close to one another in the corner of the bedroom. He was five, and I was four. We sensed something was terribly wrong by the way the older children were acting, so we kept quiet, and just watched as we hugged one another. Teddy was my best buddy, little playmate, best friend, and big brother. We were almost like conjoined twins. Now we were about to be separated from one another forever, and we had no idea what was happening.

When Mama finished packing and was set to go, she said her good-byes with short little hugs to her four soon-to-be-abandoned children.

She picked up her cardboard suitcase with one hand, baby Mary in the other arm and said, "Ana, you come wif me."

About that time, a high-pitched, shrill cry came from Tooty, "Noooooo, take me!" as she grabbed Mama's leg and hung on for dear life.

Mama just looked down and rubbed her dirty, tangled hair on the top of her little head. Then Mama looked at Opee and motioned for him to come to get Tooty. Opee came over and pried her frail little hands loose from Mama's leg. Tooty continued to sob and heave as slobber and snot were running down her pitiful little dirty face. It seemed to have little impact on Mama.

Mama pushed her glasses back up on her nose. Then she started walking toward the door; I trotted off as fast as I could to keep up with her, only looking back once to Teddy and mouthing very sadly in a low soft voice,

"Byeeeee." He pursed his lips back at me as if he were kissing me goodbye.

Mama's last words to Opee were to tell Fob that she was "going to the State of Virginia where Robby was going to help get her into a mental hospital." She said that she was about to have a nervous breakdown.

Opee didn't believe that for one minute. He was sad and felt deserted. A lump was swelling up in his throat as his eyes began to fill with tears. He swallowed the hard lump in his throat and kept watching. Poor little Tooty was crying uncontrollably as she leaned against Opee for support. Theo just stood there and stared into space. Teddy was too young to know what was going on, as he waved good-bye to me. The four children watched their mother, and two younger sisters disappear up that red clay hill. Mama, Mary, and I caught the downtown bus. Mama was walking out of the others' lives. She left them to fend for themselves against Fob.

Mama left them that day, but no one knew it would only be seven short years, and she would be gone forever.

Mama, Mary, and I were leaving the hellhole that we barely existed in, yet we called it our home. Mama was in search of a new life with Fred, in hopes of finding peace and happiness with the father of her latest child, Mary. I was extra baggage.

The four forsaken children sat on a roll-away bed for the remainder of that day wondering if Mama would come back. Discussing what would happen if she did. Worrying about how they would survive without her if she didn't.

Opee tried to be brave, mature, and strong for the younger three. Theo had nothing to offer, he depended on Opee.

Tooty continued to sob uncontrollably for her mama, wondering why her mama didn't take her too. Didn't Mama love her enough to let her go live with her too?

Teddy didn't know what was happening. He thought his best friend and little playmate would be back home in time for supper. But I would never return to the best pal I'd ever known or would ever have.

It was a very long, sad day.

When Fob came home from work, Opee faithfully did as he was told by Mama. By this time, Mama was safely far away from Fob's abuse and beatings.

"Where's ya Maw?" Fob asked.

"She's gone to Virginia; Robby's gonna get her into a mental hospital," Opee responded.

"Naw she ain't! She's off with that Fred Oder!" Fob was furious.

He used many more cuss words, but enough has been said about that; he was mad, to say the least! We don't know if he was madder because his supper wasn't on the table, or because she had left him for another man. We will never know.

As Mama, Mary, and I walked up that dusty red clay hill to catch the bus that day, Mama had high hopes of starting a new life with her new man named Fred. I had no idea that the climb up that small red clay hill was only the beginning of a huge mountain that I was to climb for the rest of my childhood while living with Fred—my new so-called stepdaddy.

The beginning of that mountain—started with a little red hill.

Fred and Mama were happy to get started with their new beginning of a life together. It was sort of like an "instant family." You know, the type where you "just add water" and *Voila!* You have a readymade family! The only difference here was, you "just add kids." It wasn't what Fred expected nor wanted.

Fred was pleased that he had won Mama over to himself and plenty glad that Mama brought along the beautiful bouncy strawberry blonde baby girl that we called Mary. Mary belonged to Fred. There was no doubt about it. Even though her birth certificate had the same last name as Fob, there was no doubt that she had Fred's blood.

What Fred didn't expect was when Mama showed up with two little girls, which included Baby Sister—that was me, Ana. Mary was easygoing, laidback, totally passive, and would let anyone run over her. Baby Sister was nothing like Mary. I was high energy, aggressive, and ten-speed ahead of everything and everyone. Nothing escaped me. I never backed down and never backed off when cornered by anyone, unless they were a lot bigger, of course. That would include Fred. To Fred, I was extra baggage.

Mary, Mama, and I met Fred downtown. There, Fred took us to the Stars and Stripes Motel where he and Mama had a quick little honeymoon. The happy honeymoon was cut a little short when I finished my first ever real shower. As I stepped out of that warm, sudsy shower, that seemed like dancing around in the rain, I dried off with a fresh, clean towel and promptly threw it on the floor. I did not know any better.

In a gruff voice, Fred said, "Pick up that towel!"

I really didn't like his tone of voice, so I responded in kind to his gruffness. "No!"

Fred said more empathically, "I said, pick up that towel!"

I reinforced my feelings too. After all, he had no authority over me. So, I once again repeated, "No!" as I tilted my head and raised my little neck at him.

Now, to get the full impact of the battle that is about to ensue, I must first describe Fred. The reader already has a mental picture of me. I was four years old and strong-willed. Fred was a tall, skinny drunk, ugly, cowardly around men, but bold toward the lesser vessels (that would include me). Fred was not going to be embarrassed in front of his soon-to-be bride, especially not because of a four-year-old little girl. So, Fred did what he had to do to get a grip with the situation. He whipped my naked little ass with his belt.

"Now, I said pick up that towel!" Fred demanded.

I reached down, picked it up, and immediately threw it back down.

The whipping commenced again. My naked flesh was burning and hot. Not as hot as my little temper! It was a battle of the Titans. After Fred had made a fool of himself with this four-year-old little girl over a towel, he finally stopped. Mama did and said nothing. And... I never picked up that towel!

What a great way to start out a new relationship with your stepchild. Funny thing, Fred never whipped his own children, but he sure whipped his stepchildren! He especially enjoyed whipping me, because I lived with him full time. He hated me, and I hated him right from the start.

This incident was just a little molehill. I jumped over this tiny hill just fine.

Little did I realize these first baby steps were just the start---up that huge mountain toward the peak that would ultimately lead to my release from the pits of my hell. I still had a long way up to go. It was a slow, tiresome climb. I still had a great deal of hell to live through, and it all laid ahead of me.

After a few days at the Stars and Stripes Motel, the happy couple found a more permanent home on Cayte Street. This little house was merely one bedroom, with a bathroom and a kitchen. It was located by a railroad track that almost ran right through the tiny backyard. A big mimosa tree graced the front yard by the front door. The tree was the only beautiful thing that could be said about the location. My little cot was just outside the kitchen door. Every morning, Mama would bring Mary and lay her in my bed. When I would wake up, Mary would be laughing because she was in bed with her big sister. I would tickle her and make faces at her to make her laugh more. She really was a sweet baby, and she loved me. From the very first day, she was my baby, I took care of her and defended her all her life.

After things cooled down between Mama and Fob, the other four children could come over for short afternoon visits. I liked this, especially getting to see my best friend and little playmate, Teddy. We were in the backyard playing with sticks, rocks, and frogs when Tooty and Theo were telling me about bumping. I knew this was something nasty, and they should not be doing it nor talking about doing it. I never tattled on them again; however, for fear that Theo might find a way to sit on my head with a pillow!

That musty smelling house needed a lot of repairs, but I guess that was all Fred could afford at the time. The bedroom door had a big hole in it, next to the doorknob. One day, I could see that the hole was plugged with a rag, so no one could see in. Of course, this arose my curiosity.

If there was something that I was not supposed to see or know about going on behind that closed door, I must check it out! There must be a secret going on in there, and I needed to know what it was!

I crept over ever so slowly. Slowly, slowly tippy-toeing, I punched out the rag in the door, so I could see in. There I saw Fred with his butt in the air, with his brown trousers still on, but pulled down below his knees, humping on Mama! I don't know how, but I knew what they were doing!

I was all of four years old, and I knew what the adults were doing in the bedroom, and my brother and sister were in the backyard talking about bumping!

Children are not born with a stamp on their foreheads that read: "Low life." They learn what they live. When they exist where life's habits are so low, crude, and stank, they rarely rise above it . . . sometimes they do---if taken out of there soon enough.

Mama's brother, Uncle Tom, lived in Mississippi. He was working in Mobile, Alabama, and staying in a boarding house during the week. While staying there, he met a woman who lived at the boarding house also and did the cooking. He thought she would make a good mate for Fob, so he introduced the two. Her name was Margaret.

Uncle Tom introduced Fob to Margaret. Fob, being uneducated and uncouth, never would pronounce words correctly, even if he knew how. So, Fob called her Marggot. You know, like a maggot, only add an "R." She looked like a maggot too; big, fat, and juicy . . . about to pop. She was a very religious person. She prayed seven or eight times a day, maybe more; it depended on how much she had sinned that day. She called it, "Staying all prayed up." She read the Bible constantly. She seemed like a nice enough lady in the beginning . . .

Well, anyway, Uncle Tom introduced Fob and Marggot, and they decided to get hitched.

Be that as it may, Fob made it perfectly clear to Marggot that he was not marrying out of love. He only needed her to cook, clean, and take care of his four children. In exchange, he would take care of her. She agreed to the arrangement. Her only demand was that he furnishes her with real toilet paper. Fob agreed. No one else could use her toilet paper. She took it with her to and from the outhouse on each of her visits. Other than that, she kept it hidden from everyone.

Mama and Fred had also decided to get married. June 25, 1955, came around and Mama and Fred sent to Wayne County, Mississippi, to the justice of the peace and tied the knot. As they were walking out of the courthouse, walking in were Fob and Marggot. What a surprise! It was a double wedding! And they lived happily ever after. Yeah! Right!

There was a problem. Marggot was the new stepmother now to Fob's four older children. She didn't like children! She had four children of her own, that she abandoned in North Carolina when she moved to Mobile. No one really knew why, just that she didn't like children. She just walked off and left her four children; so why would she agree to take on another man's four children? It didn't take long before she proved just how much she hated children. Children were a bother to her. She didn't want to care for anyone other than herself and maybe Fob.

She was constantly reporting to Fob at the end of the day (and always at the dinner table) how the children had been bad that day, and he needed to whip them. This ruined the children's dinner every night. They couldn't eat another bite after she made her nightly announcement to

Fob. Tooty and Teddy knew what was about to follow—another beating. Fob always seemed to enjoy it.

Fob beat them gladly. Marggot watched with glee while he beat Tooty and Teddy each and every night, for no known reason, other than she said, "They been bad." She was as sick minded as Fob!

"Spare the rod, spoil the child." (Prov. 13:24)

She always quoted that verse.

(That scripture was paraphrased by the ignorant people that they were.)

Fob and Marggot were married no time when Fob started showing his true colors. He thought he could knock Marggot around like he did Mama. In one of his rages, he reared back his hand to hit her. She fell down on her knees with her hands cupped up to heaven in prayer. She started calling fire and brimstone down on Fob!

"Oh, God! Please don't let Fob go to hell. He's a good man, God! I can see the flames of hell all around him! Please, God! Don't let Satan have him! Please don't strike this man down dead at this very moment! I know you have so much more good work for him to do before he dies!"

It was at that moment that Fob retreated and never hit her, *ever*. Fob was a very superstitious man.

If only Mama had the good sense to pray herself out of those terrible situations with Fob. Instead, she would curse him to hell! Then she would get the hell beat out of her by him.

After a few short months of marriage, Fob confided in the older boys that Marggot *"won't give him none."* We all know what *"won't give him none"* is. Well, good! Maybe they won't be bringing more little young'uns into this hellhole of a world to be beaten, belittled, and destroyed by their ignorant parents!

After things had cooled off a bit between Mama and Fob, Mama felt free to go over and pick up the four older children for weekend visits with us.

On one of those Friday afternoon pick-up days, it wasn't so friendly.

It all started over money. As they say, money is the root of all evil. Well, here's what happened:

Robby was in the Marines and was sending money home to Fob and Mama to help with expenses. Now that Mama wasn't living with Fob anymore, for some unknown reason, Fob didn't receive the monthly allotment check from Robby. He thought Robby must have sent it to Mama instead. Fob was insane! (Which wasn't unusual.)

Fob was blaming Mama for him not receiving the allotment check from Robby on time. He thought Mama had received it and kept it from him. Mama tried to tell Fob that she didn't have it, nor did she ever receive it. It must simply be late or lost in the mail. Fob wouldn't listen to her.

Fred stepped up to take up for Mama and said, "We don't have your check, Mr. Waterman." That was Fred's big mistake. He should have kept his boney ass in the car.

About that time, Fob grabbed Fred by the collar and slung him up against the wall and started choking him. His feet were hanging there--lifted off the floor, his knees were shaking, his eyes were bulging as he was dangling there. It was a horrible sight to see.

"I weren't talkin' to you, you wife stealin' son-of-a-bitch!" Fob was hollering.

Mama squeezed in between the two men and attempted to pull them apart. I guess Mama was trying to stop a fist blow to Fred's ugly face. She then took over the fight with words.

Mama said, "Fob, let go of him! Leave him alone!"

Fob yelled back, "You go to hell!"

Mama was on a roll when she responded, "I'll probably go to hell, and when I get there if I don't see you, I'll come back to find out where in the hell you are!"

Marggot just stood far over out of the way, praying for God to save everyone there, because they were *all* going to hell.

After Mama got Fob off Fred, all the children scurried to the car; Fred wobbled to the car with Mama's assistance. Fred was so nervous; he was shaking all over as he was making a feeble attempt at putting the keys into the ignition. Mama said, "Give me those damn keys!" She turned the key, and Fred started the car.

We could hear Fred's legs and knees hitting the inside of the car door and the dashboard when he was trying to drive off. He was trying to light his Camel cigarette, but his hands were shaking so badly he almost rammed it up his big, blackhead-plagued nose. Mama had to help him light it. Poor thing! His hands continued to shake as he attempted to drive; he could hardly shift gears. We could hear that he missed a few gear shifts and had to re-shift them once or twice. It was pitiful!

After we were clear out of sight and a good way down the road, away from Fob, Fred started to giggle in a nervous girlish sort of way and acted as if he had won the battle with Fob . . . now that he was away from him, of course! Fred was saying how he could have beaten Fob's ass had he wanted to; he was just restraining himself. On and on, he went with his big talk.

Yeah! He could have beaten Fob's ass if only Fob had let go of him. We all knew what really happened.

Fred truly didn't feel like much of a man that day on the inside, we could tell. Mama reminded him of that incident for years to come whenever she wanted to back him down.

Yeah, Fred wanted to think he was a real man; he was only a skinny coward who took advantage of women and

children. Lucky for Mama that she could back him down some of the time. Mama was the real man of the family!

7.
Trying to Climb Out of Hell / First Grade

My next home was what I thought to be a big white house on the left side corner entrance of a small subdivision. That could sound impressive, but to know the truth, it was merely a house converted into three separate apartments. We lived in the two-third bottom floor. Above us lived a young couple and their newborn infant. Also, in the same small apartment, the young girl's mother lived with them. That old lady was a full-blooded Cherokee Indian. One Easter, Mama, made the old lady a dress from scraps and bought her a new pair of cheap canvas shoes. Her old shoes were worn out with holes, and her toes hung out of them on the sides. She could barely walk because she had bad feet; she was also overweight. She had no teeth, but she would smile anyway. When Mama gave her the new frock, she cried as if no one had ever done anything for her before. From time to time, Mama would try to help those who were less fortunate than us. There was some good in my mama.

One night, the young girl came running down the outside stairs of the building and banged on our door. Her infant was sick and couldn't breathe. Mama ran up the steps, and I ran along behind her. Mama put her mouth over the baby's nostrils and sucked out some mucous, spit it out, and started again. Soon, the baby was crying and breathing again. I learned that night that newborn infants do not know how to breathe through their mouths right away; it takes a few months before they get the hang of it. I thought Mama must be some sort of nurse because she knew how to save that baby's life.

On the back side, one-third ground floor of the apartment house, there lived another young couple with no children. However, they did have a little Chihuahua dog. Sometimes, I would drop in unexpectedly for a visit. Their apartment was nothing, but one room divided by a sheet, which was hung on a wire, to separate the bedroom from the kitchen. There was another curtain that also separated the bathroom from the rest of the larger room.

Their little dog was named Twinkles. I loved that little dog. I told the young lady that I had made up a special song just for her dog. It goes like this:

"Twinkle, Twinkle, little dog,
how I wonder where you are."

I'm not so sure she believed it was an original song that I made up just for her dog. But she acted like she liked it anyway.

I loved to sing, and I was always trying to get the attention of anyone who would listen to me. Not many people did.

The young couple had an unusual car. The car's body was made of plywood and painted purple. It must have been a wrecked vehicle, and the young man made the outer body of wood and painted it. He called it his purple people eater. You know, like in that song:

"It was a one-eyed, one-horned flying purple people eater."

That was a popular song in the 1950s. I felt honored to have a real-life purple people eater in my yard. For a five-year-old little girl, the car wasn't as scary as the song made it sound.

To the left of the house was a small grocery store owned by an elderly man named Mr. Threadgill. He was so nice to me. From time to time, I would go in and charge things for Mama, and he would give me a piece of penny candy. Mr. Threadgill had the best hoop cheese around, or so I was told. He also cut fresh meat in the back of his store. We could never afford to buy his fresh meat, but Fred did enjoy his hoop cheese from time to time. I only got a teeny-weeny piece of cheese when Fred would buy a wedge. Fred ate most of it.

My older sister, Tooty, was left behind to stay with her father, Fob when our mama left Fob to marry Fred. It was in the summer of 1956 when Tooty was visiting with us for a few weeks when I had the opportunity to learn one of the most important lessons of a lifetime. We had no toys to play with, so we made do with whatever we could find. We would play *house* using old aluminum pie pans, that's what we used to make our mud pies in. Onion grass and wild plants that looked like turnip greens were cooked in them also. Pecan leaves sorta looked like fried chicken legs. Chinaberries made great pretend peas. We had all kind of things growing in our yard just waiting for us to pretend eat. Sometimes, we would act like we were "rich folks," and then we would pretend to eat proper. When we would eat like a "hobo," we would eat poorly. When Tooty told us to eat like a "Waterman," we would eat the worst of all and then laugh at ourselves! Because we were the "Watermans" that we were laughing at.

On one of those days, while we were playing house, Tooty and I went to the little store next door to buy some penny candy to add to our smorgasbord of play food. Mr. Threadgill did not come out from the meat counter promptly, so Tooty started stashing ice cream bars, cookies, and candy into her panties. It seemed like a good idea to me, so I, too, helped myself to the free goodies. Our panties were bulging. When Mr. Threadgill came out, we bought our two cents worth of candy, thanked him, and left. We ran out of the store giggling to our outdoor playhouse at the top of the hill between two sweet gum trees. We were smacking away when up walked Mama.

"What are you doing?" she asked.

Fast as a flash, Tooty said, "We just walked up here, and someone left all this stuff behind the trees."

Mama knew Tooty was lying because Mr. Threadgill called and told her that he saw us through his two-way mirror packing our panties with candy.

She made us pack up what was left of the melted ice cream, crushed cookies, and candy, then return it all to Mr. Threadgill. My apology was filled with much crying. I was so embarrassed! I cried and cried because Mr. Threadgill had been so good to me in the past, and now this was how I repaid him. I knew I had sinned. I vowed never to steal again. I learned then and there that the moment of pleasure was not worth the embarrassment of getting caught. I couldn't look Mr. Threadgill in the face for a long time. I felt as if I should have been taken to jail.

Tooty never cried---that is, not until Mama got us back to the house and beat the cold living hell out of both of us with a keen switch.

If the sorrow that I felt for having stolen from a dear, sweet friend wasn't bad enough, Mama using that keen switch on me was. I can truly say that I had rather have had the switching two or three times rather the embarrassment of having to face Mr. Threadgill with my apology. I was tainted for life at the ripe old age of five.

Keep in mind, this is the same Mama who in previous years taught her older children, by example, to steal candy and hide the wrapper behind canned goods while grocery shopping.

Oh! I forgot! It is one of the Ten Commandments:

"Thou shalt not get caught stealing."

I guess that is why we got that whipping that day.
We got caught.

To the left and up the hill from the store, was a dilapidated house that I knew for sure was haunted. One day, I slipped off to check it out. I knew everything that went on and not much went unnoticed by me. That haunted house was something that definitely needed to be investigated! As I was creeping up the rocky, red-bank hill to get a closer look at the ghost house, an old man came hobbling out, toward me, with his cane, yelling at me, "Get away from here!" It didn't take me long to do exactly as he demanded!

I ran as fast as I could, as if a ghost had approached me. At the time, I wasn't so sure that he wasn't a ghost! From time to time, I could hear yelling and screaming coming from that haunted house. Sometimes at night, I could see a small light glowing from one window. I never saw anyone come or go from there. I guess the old man died eventually because the ghost light finally went away. I wondered if the house was really haunted and if the old man was the ghost that lived in the house. Whatever the answer was, I wasn't going near that rundown, scary house again to find out.

There were a lot of things that went on while living in that big white house, or should I say apartment building, before I started first grade. Things like digging worms in the front yard and going fishing with Fred on the good days when he wasn't drunk and mad at me.

Other days, I remember going down by the nearby bridge that was located on the other side of the store. A walnut tree was growing there. One day, we picked up walnuts and cracked them. Mama made a delicious cake. Fred made fun of it and called it a sponge cake. I didn't care what he called it; it tasted good to me. We didn't get many sweets back in those days, and that cake was definitely a treat!

In July of that year, we were blessed with the arrival of a baby brother. We called him Junior. He was a sickly little fellow and demanded a lot of Mama's attention. I didn't care though; it gave Mary and me a new-real-to-life-doll to play with. We had no toys, so he was our new little toy.

At the end of the summer, right after Labor Day, it was finally time for me to become a big girl and enter first grade at Mertz Elementary School. Mama enrolled me using Fred's last name, not my (so-called) biological father's name. I went all through school with the same last name as my stepdaddy. Although it was never legally changed, for some unknown reason, no one ever questioned it. No birth certificate was ever shown nor asked for. So, I was given my stepdaddy's name. I went all through school as Ana Oder. At the time, I thought it was okay. After all, my real daddy didn't want me. At the very least, the only good thing that I can say about Fred was that he did provide food for me and allowed Mama to make my clothes from flour sacks, or from my oldest sister's old worn-out skirts.

So, the question is this: Is a bad daddy better than no daddy?

In retrospect, I think: No daddy is better than a bad daddy. I got a double dose, I had two bad daddies!

So, off I go walking to Mertz Elementary School, which was only about one mile from that big white house on Pall's Mill Road. Mama walked with me for about a week until I learned the way. From then on, I walked by myself. Again, I guess there was some good in Mama. She didn't want me to get lost.

It was around the first week of school that we started learning to write. I came home from school, so excited!

"Mama, I have learned everything!"

What I had learned that day at school was how to write "Oh." My teacher, Mrs. Smith, showed us how to make a ball to form the letter "O," then make a stick and a humpback to form the letter "h." Together they made the word <u>Oh.</u>

No one had ever taken time with me before to teach me to read and write. I thought it was amazing! However, Mrs. Smith had no idea what was ahead of her with teaching me, because I had no help at home. If I was to learn, she was to teach me everything from scratch at school. No homework was to be done at my house.

Not only did Mrs. Smith need to get me caught up academically with the rest of the children, but she also had to teach me social skills and how to respect other children. I knew nothing of these things. Respect was not a word in our house, much less what it meant. My report card usually stated that Ana does *not work well with others*. It was not long before Mrs. Smith did not like me too well. I could tell it by the way she acted toward me. Of course, this made me react to her in kind.

I guess Mrs. Smith was just an old schoolmarm, set in her ways and was going to priggishly hold to her standards no matter what the circumstance. She had no use nor patience for a nasty little girl such as me, with no manners and vulgar speech. I knew no better, and she was not taking any time to teach me any better. She did, however, take the time to stretch out my frail little hand and paddle my palm with her ruler many times. Most times, I never understood why.

The children in my class were given money to buy chocolate milk at recess. I never had that pleasure. Other treats purchased were Little Debbie cakes made of chocolate with the white eeeee's on top. Oh, how I wanted to have these yummy treats. Other children brought recess treats like apples or cookies from home. I never had that pleasure either. Sometimes, a friend might share her snack with me. I thought apples smelled especially good. We never had apples at our house.

Despite all of that, I still liked school. It was all a new adventure for me, a sort of new fresh air where people acted differently than what I had been accustomed to. I especially liked art time at school. I drew the same things every day most of the time. It was usually a picture of a white house, with a flower on each side, or maybe a tree with a seagull in flight with tulips on each side of the tree. I got my ideas from watching the other children draw.

I knew nothing about using crayons. I usually tried to eat them. I got my hand paddled for doing that too. I wondered how Mrs. Smith knew that I had eaten a crayon, maybe it was my purple colored front teeth? No, I had none of these things at my home, but it didn't take me long to fully enjoy them and figure out how to draw pretty things with them. I also liked to form funny objects out of modeling clay. I tried to eat that too, but I didn't like the taste. Besides that, it stuck to the roof of my mouth.

First grade was not easy for me, because I was behind before I got started. Even though I was a fast study, Mrs. Smith soon grew weary of me and began to be impatient with me because I could not read my Dick and Jane storybook reader. No one helped me with my homework, so I did not know those big words. During reading time, we would gather in our little circle. I must have been in the lowest reading group. Even then, I must have been the weakest reader in the lowest group.

It doesn't take the other kids long to figure out who the dummy is in the class. So, that's where it started! Kids have their hierarchy, and I was not in the top achievers, to say the least. I was just glad that Mrs. Smith didn't make me wear a pointed hat, like in the olden days, when the dummy had to wear a pointed hat and sit in the corner. She was an old schoolmarm, you know, she probably could have!

I knew the other children looked down their noses at me because I wasn't well groomed. Most of the time, my clothes were not ironed, even though we did have an iron. I had one dress that I really liked because it was store-bought. I am sure it was a hand-me-down that someone had given to me. I wore it most of the time despite the fact that it had one sleeve torn almost entirely out, and the waistband was torn loose in the back. I just pinned it up and hoped that no one would notice, but that shabby dress just got torn more and more as we played kickball outside. My mama could sew very well, I don't know why she never repaired my favorite store-bought dress. Well, torn or not, I wore it anyway. Embarrassed, yes, when the other girls made fun of me for having a torn dress. It doesn't take much criticism for a little girl like me to lose confidence in herself. Even then, I had pride in myself. I wanted to fight anyone who dared to pity me. I knew my family wasn't as well-off financially as other children's families were.

However, in my heart, I knew one day I would rise above all that scum, and I would be someone that others would respect. When I got there, I would not treat others the same way others were treating me on that day, as an average little girl, who could not help where she came from.

I had one friend whose family was in the same economic status as mine. So, if I only had one good friend, that was all it took for me to stand up against a whole room full of bullies. We stuck together for the rest of the year, and it was a very long year!

Mr. Threadgill had a young man named Paul that worked for him. Paul sacked the groceries for ladies and took them out to their cars for tips. Sometimes, he would make home deliveries in his green Volkswagen beetle-bug car that opened in the front. One day, he asked if I wanted to see it. Of course, I promptly said, yes! He took me outside and opened the front door and let me sit inside his fancy car. I liked Paul and secretly thought of him as my boyfriend, even though he was sixteen years old, and I was only six. I thought of Paul often and how sweet he was to me. He smiled at me every time I came into the store. One day, I wrote my feelings on the side of the house:

i love paul   i love paul   i love paul

I don't know how many times I wrote it, but I am sure it was more than enough to be noticed. When Fred came home from work that night, he called me into the kitchen and asked, "Who do you love?"

I said, "I love you."
Fred, "Who else do you love?"
I said, "I love Mama."
Fred, "And who else do you love?" I knew this was going somewhere . . .
I said, "I love Mary and Junior and—"
Fred, "What about Paul?"

How did he know, I wondered? I lied and said no. Then he took me outside and showed me the evidence, I knew I was in trouble. "Come in here." Then, *swoosh!* I could hear his belt rushing through the belt loops of his dirty, greasy work pants. I began to cry and beg for forgiveness. He grabbed my left arm with his left hand as he started swinging that leather belt with his right arm. Here we'd go, dancing around in circles with me screaming and jumping and Fred swinging the belt. This went on for what seemed an eternity. When it finally stopped, he told me to get a rag and clean all that filth off the side of the house. Of course, I did as he ordered. Sobbing and swearing to myself to never speak to Fred again. I don't know why he was so worried about the filth on the side of the house when he was the filthiest person that I had ever seen or would ever know!

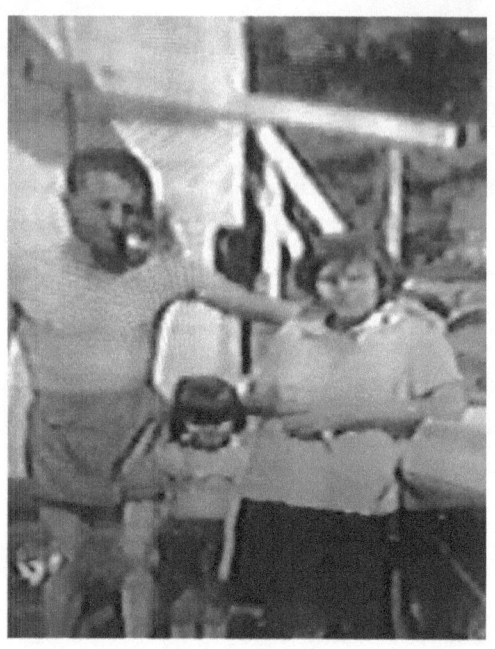

Fred, Ana, and Mama

One day, as I was walking to school by myself, I noticed that Mr. Peebles, a man who worked with Fred, was sitting on his front porch. He was a friendly and sweet sort of old man, so I stopped by and chatted with him almost daily; then I would go on my way to school. Nearly every time I would stop to visit him, he would give me an apple, which I dearly loved! So, I now had decided to visit him more often to get that apple.

Then one day, I went by his house, and he was not sitting on his porch. I rang his doorbell, there was no answer, so I walked in, as most folks did at my house. There on his dining table was his bowl of those delicious apples. I helped myself to one. After all, he had always given me one every day before, so I was sure he wouldn't mind if I took one for my recess that day. This went on for the rest of the week. I rang the doorbell, no answer, go in, grab an apple, and go to school. Until Friday of that week, when

Mr. Peebles came home and caught me in his house taking the daily apple. I explained to him that I thought it was okay since he always gave me one. Besides that, I was hungry. He said nothing, so I thought everything was fine. Fine until I saw him at our front door that night!

Mr. Peeples knocked on our front door, and I answered it. I knew right then, and there it wasn't just a friendly visit! He told Fred that his neighbor had witnessed me entering his home every day and coming out with an apple while he was not at home. At the time, I didn't think it was stealing, because he had always given me one when he was there. I cried and told him how sorry I was for having stolen from him, but I was only hungry. He told me that from now on, he would leave me an apple on his front steps if he wasn't at home to give it to me personally.

Fred said, "No! Don't do that! She can't have 'em."

As soon as Mr. Peeples left our front door and got into his car Fred lit into me! I caught mortal hell from both him and Mama that night. I don't know if they were embarrassed or what, but they sure were upset with me! All over *one little apple*! Here we go again…swinging that damn ole worn-out leather belt on me. He seemed to enjoy it. Mama just let him go on and on. "What do you mean, you were hungry, you little thief?"

My butt was burning and so was my hatred for him; that hideous looking bag of bones, he was a poor excuse for a man!

I did deserve discipline this time, but what about finding out why I was hungry? At the age of six years old, I was quickly learning about that commandment:

"Thou shalt not get caught stealing."

I really was sorry for my crime, but I missed those apples more.

After the beating, I was told to walk on the other side of the street from then on and to never take that apple from Mr. Peeples again, even if he did leave it on the front steps for me. The punishment of not getting the daily apple for recess was worse than the beating.

Is there any question that there was mutual hatred between Fred and me? I paid a high price for being the stepdaughter of Fred Oder! It was pure hell, and this was only the beginning!

We were now enjoying the brisk, cool weather of October 1957. The leaves were turning yellow and red and beginning to fall. The wind was colder, and the nights had a chill in the air; Halloween was quickly approaching. My brother Opee was living with us at that time. He told me that he was going to take me Trick-or-Treating. I had never heard of going Trick-or-Treating. I asked him what it was. He told me that we were going to get a sack and go up and down the street in our neighborhood and ask for candy. *What a great idea!* I thought. So that night, right after dark, I got my big, brown, paper grocery bag, and Opee took me up and down the streets of the neighborhood. Off we went begging for candy, and all you had to say was, "Trick-or-Treat!" The people would just hand out candy to me for free! I did not dress up in any sort of costume; I didn't know I was supposed to, so I just wore the same dress I had worn to school that day. When we were finished going from house-to-house begging for candy, Opee walked me back home to check out my stash of luscious, wonderful, tasty treats. My bag was filled with all sorts of delicious sweets and goodies, all for Mary and me to enjoy. I was about finished dividing the treats between Mary and me when I heard a knock on our front door. A large group of neighborhood kids was there Trick-or-Treating.

Opee answered the door. He told them that we were out of candy. Suddenly, I jumped up and said, "No, we're not . . . see, we still have some candy," showing them my bag of candy that we had collected.

Being embarrassed, Opee just said, "Okaaaaaayyy!" and reluctantly, he handed out all of my candy to those kids.

The rules were not clear to me at the time, but I learned them quickly when I saw that my yummy goodies were gone so fast! To this day, I am not so sure why he gave out all of my candy to those kids. Was he simply embarrassed, or was he trying to teach me a lesson? Whatever his reason, I did learn a very valuable lesson that night!

"When you treasure something, think twice before you give it away."

Christmas came around, and all the girls at school talked about asking Santa to bring them a Tiny Tears baby doll that would drink from a little plastic bottle and wet in a little diaper. That was fine and dandy but having a wet baby did not sound like much fun to me. I just remembered how much work it was to change baby Junior's diaper so often. I didn't need another wet baby to change. So, the next best thing to ask for was a tea set. I had no idea what a tea set was either.

Christmas morning came around, one little tea set was laying on the kitchen floor. No Christmas tree, just the tea set. A little metal dish, cup, and saucer tea- set to play with. Still not much fun either. I had a whole set of real dishes that I got to play with daily after supper. I got to wash them in the big nasty kitchen sink while standing on a number 2 washtub that was turned upside down. Still, not much fun either.

Just beyond the house and the store, there was a short little bridge. That bridge became my refuge from Fred. When I felt unloved or mistreated, which was often, I would go under the bridge to think. I was sort of a child troll. Sometimes, I would fish in the deep-water hole there. When I would catch a fish, Mama wouldn't cook it. She said we couldn't eat those fish because they had worms in them. I never understood why. The only way to catch a fish was to feed them with worms on a hook. So yes, they had worms in them!

One day, after having withstood another beating from Fred, I was feeling sorry for myself. I packed up my three dresses, took the iron, a cane pole, a bent baby pin (to be used as a fishhook), and some of Mama's sewing thread (to be used as fishing line). I was set to live my life as a troll under that old bridge. I had decided that I could live there and cook and eat the fish that I caught. I could walk to school from there, and no one would know or even care that I was missing. I could charge my lunch at school, as I most often did in the past. Mr. Threadgill would surely give me credit at his store if I got hungry. Mama would never care, or ever miss me! I had decided that day, then and there, that my mama did not love me. If she had, she would have never taken sides with Fred every time there was a squabble between us. Surely, if Mama loved me, she would have taken up for me once-in-a-while when Fred beat me. But no, she never did. She just let him have his way with me . . . beating after beating . . . for what seemed to be for no good reason.

So, there I was, in my new runaway home, on the creek bank, sitting under the bridge on my little lard bucket (which was used to hold my fishing worms). I was pondering my future and just fishing away with my little cane pole, thread, a bent baby pin, and worm. I was just about to get a bite when I looked up and . . .

Lo and behold! (Lo and behold was an old family expression.) there stood Mama! I froze on my little lard bucket! Actually, I think I nearly messed in my britches!

"What are you doing?" she said inquisitively with a sort of smirk/half smile on her face.

"I am running away from home, because no one loves me and I hate Fred," I told her.

"What are you going to eat?" she asked.

"I am going to fish and cook'em and eat'em on a campfire like a hobo."

"What are you going to do with my iron?"

"Iron my dresses," was my quick response.

"Where are you going to plug in the iron?"

Well, I hadn't gotten that far yet.

She told me I couldn't stay there, so I packed up my duds, and we walked back to the house before Fred got home and found out what I had done. I was glad that Mama didn't tell him about this one. Mama never said she was sorry that I felt unloved. Mama never hugged me and welcomed me back home. She just said I couldn't stay there under the bridge. I guess I wasn't cut out to be a child troll or hobo. At the time, being a runaway child troll seemed like a better idea than living there with Fred!

I still think it was a better idea!

Another time, after Fred had taken his rage out on me and I was feeling sorry for myself, I had decided to write to my oldest brother Robby and ask for help. By this time, Robby was in the service and lived far away. I was sure that if he knew how I was being treated that he would come and rescue me. Tooty was again visiting with us for the weekend. I could not write as well as she could. She knew how to write those big words that I could not spell. So, I asked for her help in constructing the letter. We composed a letter to Robby and told him how mean and bad Fred was to me and could he please come to get me to go and live with him. I did not know his address, so I had to employ the help of Mama. I asked if she might put my letter in the envelope with her letter the next time she wrote to Robby. She said she would.

Everything was fine until Fred got home that night.

"You think Robby is going to come save you from me?" he said.

I froze in my tracks. I knew then and there that Mama had shown my letter to Fred, and he had read it. Why did my mama betray my trust and give away my most secret thoughts, fears, and hopes of reaching out for help? Why could she have not just talked to me about it? She sided with Fred again, against me.

Fred again took off his belt, left hand, my left arm, around and around we went. Beating me until I could cry no more. "Now that's what you get for telling lies on me!"

Do you think I ever told on Fred again? **Hell no!**

No one would ever believe me!

If getting beatings from Fred were unbelievable, do you think even worse things would be believed?

How could I ever tell of worse things? I might be killed for telling of those worse things.

Those worse things only happen to bad little girls, so I thought back then.

First grade was the longest nine months of my life thus far. Finally, the year was coming to an end, and I was passing with squeaking-by grades. I do not know who was gladder to be rid of the other, me, or Mrs. Smith.

At last, the summer was approaching, and new adventures were just waiting for me to explore and experience.

One exciting experience happened very soon that summer. It was the first grass cutting of the year. Mama had the lawn mower going in the high grass in the backyard. There was a clack-idy-clack sound from under the mower. Mama reached down to remove an old rusty clothes hanger from getting farther caught in the mower. About that time, the mower caught the rest of the hanger and whipped it around, cutting off Mama's right thumb! Blood was spurting everywhere! Mama was a tough old biddy; she never screamed. She just turned off the mower, came into the house and wrapped it with a rag to stop the bleeding. Someone took her to the doctor to have it sewn up.

When she came home, my brother Opee was outside looking for the rest of her thumb. He found it and brought it in. Of course, it could not be sewn back on in those days. Opee wanted to keep it in a little medicine bottle with alcohol as a souvenir.

Mama said, "absolutely not! If you keep my thumb, I'll cook it in your biscuit one morning!" The thumb was not kept. Mama was still able to use that injured nub of thumb for anything she wanted or needed for the rest of her life.

In August of that summer, we got another surprise, another baby sister! We called her Ginger. She was a beautiful baby and a good baby. She wasn't sickly and wheezy like baby Junior.

On the day that Mama brought her home from the hospital, something extraordinary happened. I must say I truly enjoyed watching this event go down.

It happened this way:

My beautiful, eldest sister, Ellen, was working and living with us at the time. She had a regular paying job and had saved enough money to afford a beautiful, pink Pontiac car. (It helped to have a boyfriend who sold cars.) She usually got off work later in the day, after I got home from school, but today was different.

Mama was in the hospital for a couple of days with the delivery of our new baby sister, so when Mama finally arrived back home with our little bundle of joy, I was ready for the happy occasion. The only problem was, it wasn't so happy. Like I said, today was different.

I do not know where I had been for those few days, probably staying with a relative. When I arrived back home, I noticed that Ellen's pink Pontiac was already in the yard. She must have gotten off work early to see our new baby, I concluded. I anxiously ran into the bedroom to see the new baby too. There stood Ellen beside Mama's bed. Ellen looked absolutely gorgeous, as usual! But today she was unusually beautiful! She had on a pale pink, tight, pull-over sweater that showed off her 36-C breasts, which came to high points through her sweater. She also had a black silk scarf tied around her neck, a grey poodle skirt, and a black shiny leather belt pulled tightly around her thin little waist. She looked even more elegant in her black pointed (really) high heels. This pretty lady did not match the scene I was about to witness.

Anyway, I ran into the bedroom just in time to see Mama lying in bed, holding the baby and smoking a cigarette. Fred was sitting to the left side of the bed, stinking, with his head hung low, not saying a word, and smoking also. I could smell his sweaty stench as I entered the room! A bottle of Four Roses whiskey was sitting on the bedside table, almost empty. I could see that Fred's eyes were bloodshot whenever he would look up. Ellen and Mama were talking in a not-so-friendly voice, to put it very mildly!

Mama: "Fred said while I was in the hospital, you came and got into bed with him!"

Ellen: "That's a lie!"

Ellen: "Fred, tell Mama, that's a lie!"

Fred said nothing. He just sat there smoking his Camel cigarette with his nervous, shaking hands. His greasy head hung low with a stinky sweat pouring from his forehead that was covered with blackheads.

Mama: "Get yor stuff and get out!" As she put out her Camel cigarette, she attempted to rise with the baby in her arms, but pain caught her in her stomach, so she sat back down on the bed.

Ellen pleaded, "Mama, don't make me go! Fred told you a lie!"

"I told you to get yor stuff and get out, you little hussy!" Mama said in a louder voice, using much more authority than before.

This scenario went on for several minutes with Fred doing and saying nothing. He was not looking at either woman, just looking down, guiltily. It was obvious he had been drinking to the point of getting totally drunk and was very nervous about the whole situation.

Now keep in mind, Ellen was one of the most beautiful women in the county in those days. She could have any man of her choosing. Ellen was approximately five feet, five inches tall, and weighed around 110 pounds. Her waist was all of twenty-one inches. She had long black hair, crystal blue eyes, and sparkling white teeth. So, the question is this: Why would she want to go to bed with a greasy, stinky, rotten-tooth, good-for-nothing piece of dirt like Fred?

I often saw Fred staring at Ellen in a vulgar sort of way. At my young age, I should not have known what those looks meant, but I knew all too well. I believe he was visualizing himself raping her.

It was a figment of Fred's imagination (and fantasy) if they ever went to bed together! He made all this story up just to make Mama jealous. It worked. Fred would love to have gone to bed with Ellen and have sex with the most beautiful woman in Mobile County. His sick mind was working overtime in this case! He should have kept his evil thoughts to himself, instead of trying to make Mama jealous. What a fool he was!

Ellen had heard enough of all this nonsense. She took her stance more firmly than before with both hands on her hips then screamed it out once more, "Fred, why did you want to tell Mama such a lie? Tell Mama the truth! You know good and well that none of that shit ever happened! I oughta whip your ass, you worthless, stinky ass, sack o shit!" (I told you Ellen had a vulgar mouth!)

Fred still said nothing, by now, he is nervously shaking at his knees as he looked up at Ellen with a scared-to-death look on his ugly-mug face. The drunken fool should have been scared to death and getting nervous as hell too by now!

Mama screamed again at Ellen, "Get out, or I'mma gonna—"

Ellen didn't listen to Mama, nor did she obey. Still standing quite firm, she swiftly and unexpectedly walked over and slapped the soup . . . no, Ellen knocked the stew . . . no, Ellen beat the shit out of Fred! (Sorry for using that word, but she did!)

Right before my very eyes! She gave Fred one full-handed, full-faced, teeth-shattering blow to his head that brought him to the floor, crying like a baby. He fell out of the chair, breaking it, knocking over his whiskey bottle, and damn near bit his Camel cigarette in half. I think he might have swallowed it!

Ellen said: "Now that's what you get for telling lies about me!"

Then she added: "And this is what you get for drooling every time you look at me!"

With that being said, Ellen gave him a swift hard kick in his skinny ass while he was still on the floor. I don't remember how many times she kicked him with those pointed toe high heel shoes, but she was furious, and she took it out on him with a vengeance. There was a great deal of rage pinned up in Ellen from past years of beatings that she received from Fob and Mama. Now was her comeuppance for all those wrongs committed against her with that damned old chap belt! It all poured out on Fred!

Ellen had learned to slap and fight from the very best of 'em . . . Mama! She had been physically abused all of her life. Now that she was grown, it was payback time!

Needless to say, I loved every minute of watching all of that! I hated Fred, and I thought Ellen was a heroine.

After having made her point, Ellen then walked across the hall and packed her things to leave. Despite having nowhere to go, she left anyway.

I hated to see Ellen pack up her few belongings to leave us that day, but Mama was insistent that she had done wrong. Mama took up for Fred and not her child once again. One reason I hated to see Ellen go that day was that when she was around, Fred never slapped me or talked mean to me. He was always on his best behavior. I thought of Ellen as my protector. I knew she loved me and would take up for me against Fred. I dearly loved my beautiful big sister! I cried as I watched her drive away, she was crying too.

I think Mama really knew the truth about Fred. However, I think Mama felt trapped in her life and needed him to take care of her. It was as if she had no way of taking care of herself.

Maybe Mama just felt beaten down and had decided not to get back up. . .

You know, like a dog in a dogfight that has lost the fight. The dog has fought and has given all it can give. It has been beaten down and gotten up. Again, beaten down and gotten back up. After a while, that dog decides there is no use in getting up anymore. Just stay down, where it is safe and less painful.

Maybe that is why Mama stayed in those bad situations and just laid low. She too was a victim. So sad!

8.
Maybe There Is a Heaven / Second Grade

> *Just when life seems dark and dim with no way out of hell, God sends a little angel to let you know that,*
> *"Yes, Ana, I do care for you!"*

I entered second grade at Raphael Sims Elementary School when I was seven years old. I was small and skinny for my age. To say that I was undernourished would be mildly spoken. My teeth were in very bad condition. I had a toothache almost every day. I thought that an abscess was normal. Mama would give me an aspirin from time to time to put on the tooth to help with the pain. Sometimes it would help, sometimes not. Don't get me wrong, we had a toothbrush in our house, but no one ever used it. I was never taught to clean my teeth daily. Sometimes, I would see the adults chewing on a frayed sweet gum tree twig to clean their teeth while talking under a tree in the afternoon. That was the extent of my knowledge of teeth cleaning.

It was 1958. I was anxiously awaiting to catch the big yellow school bus that would take me downtown to meet my new teacher. Little did I know that she would be my guardian angel. I was waiting in the front yard on the corner of the street when the big rusty bus came puttering down the street. My heart began to pound harder and harder! I had never ridden a school bus, and today was the day! It didn't matter to me that my dress had a hole in the back and my shoes were worn and dirty. I really didn't notice all of that at the time. I was just excited to get started back in school. I liked school. The school was a safe haven for me, a safe place to get away from Fred's big slapping hands and piercing eyes.

My new teacher was young and pretty. She had long golden-brown hair that she wore pulled back in a ponytail. Her name was Mrs. Smith, another Mrs. Smith. This new Mrs. Smith liked me, and I liked her right from the start. I could tell it was going to be a good year for me.

Mrs. Smith had a slightly mentally challenged son who was also in our class. His name was Bucky. I couldn't help but like him, because he was so sweet to me. I did not make friends easily because we moved around so often. I really did not have good social skills nor good manners. Mama would not allow us to play with other children, just one another, or our cousins, so how was I to know how to speak or have good manners? Bucky knew no difference; therefore, he liked me for who I was. We had no comparisons to worry about with one another.

Because I did not make friends easily, I became special friends with Bucky. Not because he was the teacher's son, but because he gave me a chance. I tried to always be sweet and friendly to Bucky. I could always make him laugh. Bucky was big and goofy looking. Other kids made fun of him, but I didn't. I knew how bad it felt to be made fun of and bullied. Somehow, I knew it wasn't a good thing to be mean to others less fortunate than you. I also knew that if it were not for the grace of God, I too could have been born mentally retarded, or something much worse.

Mrs. Smith took time with me. She kindly and gently corrected some of my bad habits and vulgar speech. She made me want to please her. Never did she ever once spank my hand with a ruler and make me cry. I never got into trouble with her. I felt like she loved me and cared about me; I don't know why. It was easy for me to love her in return. I always tried to please her and do my best work for her. She would always brag on me when I did well. No one else in my life ever did that.

Mrs. Smith was very kind to me. She knew that I had bad teeth and had pain every day. She wanted to take me to the dentist. One night, she came unexpectedly to our little apartment house to talk to my mama about letting her take me to the dentist. She explained that she would pay for all the costs. Mama's pride got in the way of good dental care for her child. She immediately told her it was none of her business and told her to leave. My heart sank as I watched the most beautiful lady that I knew and loved driving her nice big car out of our front yard and down the street. Tears began to swell up inside of my throat; not because of my loss of good dental care, but because my sweet, caring teacher was humiliated for her attempted good deed.

The abscesses continued, and my teeth continued to rot and fall apart.

After seeing firsthand, the squalor in which we lived, Mrs. Smith became even closer and sweeter to me than ever before. She took a special interest in me and helped me to want to learn. She helped me get my homework done before I went home. I guess she knew I would get no help once at home.

Mrs. Smith also loved horses. She rode her horse in the Mardi Gras parade that year; I saw her. I was so impressed! I felt like I knew a celebrity. In a way, she was more important than a celebrity---to me anyway. She made sure that she threw me lots of trinkets from her big beautiful brown horse.

I always admired the majorettes in the Mardi Gras parades. I wanted to be a majorette so badly! I dreamed about me with my little head held high, leading the group, twirling my little baton in a flashy beautiful costume.

Surely, if I were a majorette, the other girls would like me and have respect for me. I wanted that dream to come true. Maybe if I wished upon a star long and hard, it might come true. Or what if I found a four-leaf clover, would it bring me good luck and my wish would come true?

Christmastime came around again. Santa always seemed not to leave much at our house in the past years. Maybe only one thing if anything, I remember from the years before. I received a little tea set from last year. This year was different! When Tooty and I woke up on Christmas Day, we went into the kitchen to find that there were toys, dolls, candy, fruit, and a Christmas tree all lit up! There were toys for all of us. Toys that I had never seen before nor after. Surely, there was a Santa Claus! I know in my heart of hearts that it was Mrs. Smith who left the toys on our front porch the night before without her presence being known nor a word spoken. What an angel she was. God bless you, Mrs. Smith, wherever you are.

In the spring of the year, our school celebrated a Spring Festival. The theme that year was *The Circus*. What do you think Mrs. Smith's class was assigned to do? The girls were majorettes! I was so excited! Mrs. Smith asked my mama if I could participate. Mama agreed to make my costume since she was a good seamstress. The costumes were little red round flared skirts. Red tops with white horizontal stripes and buttons. The hats were round oatmeal boxes covered in white fabric. Somehow, I obtained little white boots to top off the attire. I am confident that Mrs. Smith bought them for me.

Mrs. Smith asked me to be the head majorette. This meant that I would lead the rest of the girls into the arena and around in a circle twirling our little batons for all to adore.

While practicing for this big event daily at playtime, I got one of my first lessons on "little bitches." I was trying to lead my class of little girls in the drill. I did not have confidence as you can imagine; therefore, I was not doing a great job of leading the march. One of the pretty, smart, popular girls, whose name I will never forget; Lisa, who started to criticize me. Lisa had long curly, shiny blonde hair that smelled of perfumed shampoo. Not of Octagon soap, like I was accustomed to using, which caused my hair to cast a dull finish with an odd odor.

The criticism coming from Lisa was humiliating, to say the least. It turned from criticism to making fun, then it turned into mocking me because I could not march in a straight line. I cried because of the humiliation from the group, which she was the ringleader. The truth is, Lisa wanted to be the head majorette. She humiliated me, and I succumbed to her.

I went to Mrs. Smith and asked to be removed from the position of honor. I told Mrs. Smith that I did not want to be the leader any longer. She asked, "why?" I told her that I thought Lisa could do a better job. Mrs. Smith said if she thought Lisa could have done a better job, she would have asked Lisa to do it the first place.

Again, I asked her to remove me and ask for Lisa to have my position as the head majorette. I never told Mrs. Smith what Lisa had done or the mean things she said to me.

I was happy to just blend in with the rest of the girls where no one would make fun of me. No one would know if I messed up or not. After all, my mama wasn't there to see me march anyway, so what did it matter? No one was there to be proud of me, except Mrs. Smith. Later that evening, Mrs. Smith told me how good I looked on the field and what a great job I had done marching in the school parade. Compliments like that were never spoken around my house. I still remember her sweet comments today.

After that evening of fame and glory, do you think Lisa was grateful that I turned over my position to her? Do you think she was my friend? No.

I am sure that characteristic in that little girl went with her for the rest of her life.

Bitch theory:
"Get what you want by any means possible and walk on whomever you have to in order to get there."
Warning: Bitchy little girls make bigger bitchy women.

I imagine today that same <u>little</u> girl is all grown up and is in the Junior League in some <u>little</u> town, bossing around the other <u>little</u> ladies and thinking she's a *<u>big shot</u>*. Poor <u>little</u> girl!

Mother's Day was in May of 1958. Mrs. Smith helped her class make Mother's Day cards for each of our mothers. She had an instant Kodak camera. She took all our pictures; I patiently waited in line to have my photograph made. I posed shyly with my hands behind my back. My hair was pulled back neatly in a ponytail. I wore the cutest dress that I owned; my mama made from flour sacks. A hedge of honeysuckle graced the old picket fence behind me in the picture. My picture turned out pretty good, I thought. However, Mrs. Smith thought it wasn't quite good enough, and she needed another photo-shot of me. She asked me to pose for another shot. I now know that she wanted a picture of me for herself.

I love you, Mrs. Smith. Only you and God know who you are and what you did for that little needy child in second grade, at Raphael Sims Elementary School, 1958. You were an angel to me.

Ana's Mother's Day card, second grade

9.
Turning Up the Fire of Hell / Third Grade

Author's note:

It has been several years since I last picked up writing the story of my life. For some strange reason, I have not wanted to write about this part of my life. It is a portion that has long since been buried in the black- back-segments of my mind. I lived through it and made myself stronger because of my horrible experiences. I try not to visit those areas of my mind too often because of the pain it causes. Today when I think back on those days, I hurt for that little girl who no longer exists. I hurt for the little girl who could do nothing to help herself out of a bad situation. I hurt for the little girl who was crying out for help to so many people in so many ways. No one really seemed to have taken her hints or taken her serious. She was only a child. What sort of messages was she sending out with those little covert words? After all, molestation doesn't happen to "good little girls!" "Bad little girls" ask for it! And so, it goes on . . . 19.7 percent of us good little girls keep our silence and suffer therein. Therein is the shame, because we think no one will care, or listen, or much less dare to believe such things could really be true.

I don't know why we moved away from Pall's Mill Road as soon as I finished second grade. But I do remember waking up one morning on the front porch of Navajo Road. My younger sister, Mary, was sitting beside me on the rusty, green, metal glider. It wasn't our glider, just a glider that the previous tenants had left behind. We were glad they did, for we made good use of it. The earthy smell of wet pine straw or moss or something was in the air. I had never smelled it before. Sometimes today I smell that same earthy, mossy odor, and it takes me back to that exact place and time—on the front porch with sweet little Mary, just gliding away, without a care in the world . . . most days.

Our new home was a place where a little white house stood with three large, fuchsia azalea bushes beautifying the front yard. A pine straw driveway was lined with plum trees. In the spring, the plum trees were full of beautiful light pink blossoms. I knew luscious plums were to follow that summer. I would usually eat the plums before they were ripe.

This sounds nice and homey, doesn't it? It was simply a rented little four-room house with a detached carport in the backyard. Our septic tank always overflowed in the backyard and could be smelled for several houses away, year-round.

It seemed for a while, Mama took pride in our new home, and she kept it clean. The windows were always up while the freshly mopped floors were drying. However, I don't remember the bathtub ever being clean. It always had a dark, thick yellow ring around it. As a child, I thought this was normal. One day, I took a razor blade and scraped all the scum off the tub. Amazingly, it was bright white. When Fred came home, I proudly showed it to him, in hopes of getting a compliment. His only comment was, "That's the way you should keep it." I never scraped it clean again. I didn't want that to be one of my other many chores!

It was a crisp, early summer day, I was sitting on the front porch with Mary in our favorite green glider. My brother, Opee, and Mama were also out there. Opee was singing and playing his guitar for our entertainment. I thought Opee could play and sing quite well. As Opee was singing, Mama looked up, and there was an old colored man moseying down the road. Mama hollered for the old guy to come over. "Hey. Hey you boy, come here." The old man slowly, reluctantly walked over our way. We all smiled, and all seemed to be going well. Mama asked him if he could play the guitar. He said he could play "jus' a little." So, he proceeded to entertain us with a song or two. Then Mama said to him, "Can you play the Nigger Blues?"

"Nome, I don't know nothin' 'bout playin' no nigger blues," the old guy said very humbly as he handed the guitar back to Opee and stood up. Mama laughed as she and Opee walked into the house. Opee lowered his head and shook it sadly in dismay at Mama's mean actions toward the humble colored man. I could tell Opee felt bad for the old man's humiliation.

The old guy then slowly walked off in the same direction in which he was headed before Mama interrupted him. I was watching as he left. I knew he was embarrassed by what Mama had said to him, although I wasn't for sure why.

I ran after him. "Hey, mister. Mister!"

He turned around, "Yes, little lady?"

"Don't be sad 'cause you don't know no 'nigger blues' song. Mama don't know it neither. If you ever learn it, you come back, and I'll sing it with you. Besides, Mama can't even sing! I've heard her try to sing. I <u>can</u> sing, and I'll help you!"

The old guy sort of laughed and smiled at me and said, "Well, thank ya, I'll jus do that! You go on yor way now, little lady, 'for you get in trouble with ya momma."

We both smiled at one another and departed. I never saw that kind, old gentleman again.

If that humble old man only knew what a mean hellcat my mama was, he would have never answered her summons to come to our front porch that day!

I was in third grade, and my new front teeth were fully extended. I was now bucktoothed! I was little and skinny, so this made them look even bigger. I was embarrassed about the way I looked. The boys called me Bucky Beaver. I had learned by now to use a wash rag and wipe off my front teeth to make them appear to be clean. At least the yellow slime wasn't apparent. My back teeth were still in very bad condition. My only hope was for my permanent teeth to come in and replace the old rotten ones.

One day, we were visiting Mama's sister, Aunt Sweetie Pie. As I was talking with her, I was covering my mouth with my hand; she took notice. Being the kind and gentle lady that she was, she simply said, "Ana, smile for me."

Embarrassingly, I did as she requested. I gave her one big bright-eyed, full-face smile, exposing all four of my newly acquired ivory tusks.

She said, "Suga Foot, you have a beautiful smile and a pretty little face to go along with it." No one had ever noticed that about me before, much less ever said such a thing!

Then she said, "You know, when I was a little girl your age, my teeth outgrew me too!" We both laughed as I recovered my new ivories, which were all sprouted in four different directions. Then she added, "You know what I did to fix the problem?"

"*No! What?*" I was quite curious for the solution to my elephant-like tusk appearance . . . that I was sure, I'd be stuck with for the rest of my life.

She said, "I wore rubber bands around my front teeth to pull them together. Maybe you should try it too!"

What a great idea! We immediately went into her kitchen to find a rubber band. She showed me how to wind it around my front teeth several times tightly in order to pull them together. I now had homemade braces for my teeth. I wore a rubber band on my front teeth day and night every day for about a year, or until my teeth came together in the front. I never wore the rubber band to school because I knew the kids would surely find another way to make fun of me! There is no telling what they could have made of that!

I can just hear them now . . . "Ana, Ana, rubber bands, and bananas." Or something like that, maybe something worse! I am sure they would have come up with something. I wasn't giving them any ammunition to use against me this time!

Some kids are just plain hellions!

Mama loved to sew. She could make a dress just by looking at a Sears-Roebuck catalog. All our clothes were homemade. Usually, our dresses were made of flour sack material, or maybe from Ellen's flared-tail skirts that she no longer wore. Mama was good at recycling and making the most of things. I never had store-bought panties. My panties were bloomers that matched my dresses. I was embarrassed if my dress blew up and someone saw my underwear. One time, a girl asked me, "What was that under your dress?" I lied and told her I had on shorts. I always wanted to be like the other girls, but I never had the things they had, and I never could dress as well as they. But I tried to hold my head up and have some sort of pride despite where I came from. If anyone felt sorry for me, I would make excuses. If they made fun of me, I wanted to beat 'em up! Of course, that never happened, but I wanted to.

    I was fortunate that Mama could sew. She entered a crossword puzzle contest and won a new pink electric Atlas sewing machine. We thought we were really uptown now! Mama made all of us girls pastel ruffled organza dresses for Easter that year. I was all decked out in pink. Mary wore mint green; Ginger was in white and Tooty wore lavender. We were all scrubbed clean as a whistle with shiny pink noses and excited about going to church on Easter Sunday. We pulled up in front of Eastside Baptist Church, where Fred's mother and father were members. When we arrived at the church, we were told to "just go in." Mama and Fred refused to go in. I don't know why. I guess they got into a fuss or something. One thing was for sure, Fred was not a churchgoer.

    It was a well-known fact that Fred was the black sheep of his family. Big Mama and Granddaddy Oder did not approve of his way of life, and neither did they approve of his drinking. They certainly did not approve of my mama. They thought of her as an older divorced woman with seven other children who obviously seduced their son into marrying her. It was the truth, but he was no catch either! That filthy, rotten-toothed, blackhead-faced, hellhound of a man was good for nothing! Mama was eleven years older than Fred. My mama's name was Gertrude, but she started calling herself Lucille when she married Fred. I guess she changed her name because she wanted a fresh start in life. I am not so sure she got what she was hoping for. She got a change in her life, but I am not so sure it was any better, it was just a change. The beatings changed only slightly. My so-called, real father, Fob, did not drink regularly, as did Fred. He didn't have to; he would just get himself mad for any ole reason, and then he would beat up on Mama or any kid in sight. Mama jumped out of the skillet into the fire. Fred drank himself sick every weekend, and then he would slap Mama around. Mama had a tendency for violence. Therefore, she could defend herself against Fred. He was a cowardly, skinny man so she could back him down, but not before he could get in a few good licks. He was a hellish, worthless bully to women and children. I hated him.

It was another one of those drunken weekends. It all started out so happy. We had tomato sandwiches and Coke-a-Cola for supper. Fred had his Four Roses whiskey that he drank until it was gone. The more he drank, the meaner he would get. Usually, he and my older brother Opee would play the guitar and sing. The children watched Saturday night westerns. To keep Fred from being mean, I would request songs that I knew he liked to sing. He could not sing, but he enjoyed picking the guitar and trying to sing.

You see, children who are abused learn to be pleasers to protect themselves. This is a pure example of such. As the night grew longer, his eyes would wallow back and forth before falling out of his chair and peeing on himself. And that was the end of a good Saturday night at my house, because he didn't beat me, or at least slap me around.

One day, I walked home from school, and a strange car was in the pine straw driveway. I ran inside to find a nice man talking to Mama. Our Liberty National Insurance man was there collecting his monthly premium of twenty-five cents per child for burial insurance. Mama faithfully paid it on time because he came around to collect. She was telling him about what had happened the prior weekend while we were all in Mississippi visiting with her parents.

It was unclear to me what she was telling him. While we were away, Fred was home alone, in his usual drunken state. The next-door neighbor's fifteen-year-old daughter came over and asked if she might use our telephone. The girl was tall and pretty. Her name was Barbara Island; we called her Bobby. There were four Island girls: —Paula, Barbara, Pam, and Donna.

Bobby had called her friend's number, but the line was busy; she was waiting to call her back. While she was waiting, Fred tried to force her into his bedroom. She ran home and told her parents. They called the police and filed a report. Mama took Fred's side, once again, by saying that he had to go to the bathroom, and he was only trying to move her out of his way. I knew right away that was not the truth, nor his real intentions! Fred was attempting to rape that young girl, and I knew it!

The Island family never let me play with their little girls again. I was from a bad family. At the time, I did not understand why. I had done nothing wrong, so why was I being punished? I now know why. Mrs. Island was only protecting her daughters from Fred by not letting us play together any longer. Until that horrible incident happened, Mrs. Island was very kind to me. Now I had lost my best friend and playmate, Donna. We were in the same third-grade class at Morningside Manor Elementary School.

The Islands were a military family that moved next door to us, they previously lived in Anchorage, Alaska. I was so impressed with this family. They had a tiny travel trailer, which they kept parked next to their carport. Some Saturday mornings, Mrs. Island would prepare lunch and invite me over to dine in their travel trailer with Donna and Pam. Kool-Aid, sandwiches, chips, or maybe a cookie were such a treat to me. Occasionally, if I was at their house doing homework with Donna, she would ask me to stay for supper. That was the first time I had eaten rice with milk and sugar. It was so good! Some kids just don't know how good they have it!

I loved to play with their conch shell. I was told that if you put it up to your ear, you could hear the ocean. You really could hear something! I thought it really was the ocean. I listened to it every time I went to their home. My visits to the Island home were the first time I experienced how real family life should be. You know, where the father and mother love each other, and that love is shown toward the children. At mealtime, everyone sits down and talks happily about the day at school or work. No screaming or physical fighting, no mean looks from across the room. Some kids just don't know how lucky they are to be born into normal families! Lord! I missed playing with Donna and being in her normal home!

It happened on another drunken Saturday afternoon that my real hell on earth all started! Mama wasn't at home. She must have gone to buy groceries. All four of us little ones were watching television while sitting on the floor. I looked across the room at Fred, he was sitting on the couch with his nasty, stinky feet up, and he was picking that green stuff out from under his toenails. I could smell that sharp stench of his feet from across the room. He had on his sleeveless ribbed undershirt; the smell of his sweat was unbearable. His pants were on, but his belt buckle was unfastened and the belt hanging loose. He had an evil-vulgar look in his eyes as his stares were penetrating me. I felt like roadkill, and a buzzard was about to devour my dead flesh. I just can't explain the feeling that was going on in my sick stomach! His bloodshot eyes were just glaring at me. His eyes looked at me, then he darted his eyes toward his bedroom . . . he looked at me, darted his eyes toward his bedroom again. He was talking to me with his eyes. I knew he was telling me to go to his bedroom. He got up and went to his bedroom, and I was supposed to follow. I did, like a little obedient lamb being led to slaughter.

It was a rare occasion that Fred was ever nice to me. Now he was acting nice because he was going to sweet talk me into the unspeakable.

"Do you love me?"

"How much do you love me?"

"You don't love me."

"How can you prove you love me?"

"If you loved me, you would . . ."

These are the subtle ways of opening the door into molestation. Slow, sweet conversation followed by slow, easy touches. All of this is unsuspecting at first, especially to an inexperienced nine-year-old little girl. Nothing usually happens the first time. Everything is over; everyone seems happy, nothing goes reported, because nothing happened. Next time, it is the same song, second stanza!

Did I tell my mama about this first encounter? No. Because I thought Fred had finally decided to be nice to me. I thought he had finally decided not to hate me. When you are nine years old, you want so badly for your parents to approve of you and love you. I was glad for any moment of niceness from him. To me, being nice was anything other than slapping me, looking at me with those disdaining eyes, or yelling at me. Little did I know what his form of niceness meant for me later! The next time, it was the same song, third stanza.

Next time, same song, forth stanza.

Next time. . . Oh! God! Please. . . not that same song again!

It was on a beautiful, sunshiny summer day. Mama was hanging out clothes on the rusty sagging clothesline. I can still see it today; two long lines of wire were being held up by a one-inch-by-four-inch board. All sorts of laundry were hung together—towels, colored and whites, pants, dresses, etc. It didn't matter much, what got washed with what, as long as everything got washed and dried before nightfall.

While Mama was busily going about her chores of hanging out the laundry, she told me to go inside and check on my baby brother, Junior, who was inside alone. Not wanting to stop playing, I back talked to her with a childish remark, "I wish he would just die!" When I said that, Mama started running toward me at full speed. I knew then, and there I was in for a whipping! What I did not know was, I was in for the beating of my life!

I ran as fast as I could down the street, screaming, "Somebody help me! There's a crazy woman after me! She's gonna kill me!" Even then, as a little girl, I knew my mama was not totally sane. We all walked on eggshells around her. The problem was that day, I forgot to walk on those eggshells and boy did I pay!

When I started my rant of running down the street, begging for help, Mama stopped chasing me and disappeared into the house. She closed the door, turned down the shades, and waited for me to return. Just as a black widow spider sits in her tangled web and waits for her prey in perfect, still silence---so was the scene I was about to return to.

I finally stopped running and pleading for help when I realized that no one was going to come to my rescue. I slowly walked back toward the house and climbed into a tree and waited until I thought the coast was clear. Several hours passed. I thought surely by now she had forgotten about it, cooled off, and had forgiven me. I was wrong. I walked into the house with a shy remorseful look with my head hung low. Before I could ask for forgiveness, she grabbed me and dragged me back outside and tied me to the carport post. A tree limb was waiting. There she beat me and beat me. I don't mean she beat me with a switch, it was a big tree limb. It drew blood all over my body. I was screaming and wiggling around and around that metal post! It seemed like forever!

Mama was huffing and puffing, swinging that limb crazily and screaming at me while frothing at the mouth, "You gonna ever do that again? Huh? Huh? You ever gonna say that again? Huh? Huh? You ever gonna run down the street again? Huh? Huh?" On and on . . .

"No, Mama! No, Mama! I promise, Mama! Just stop, Mama! I'll never do it again, Mama! Please stop, Mama! I love you, Mama!" I begged her for mercy from the concrete floor of the carport as I looked up into her raging, red eyes. It was as if I was looking into the eyes of the devil himself!

"What'da ya mean there's a crazy woman after ya? Huh? Huh? You ever gonna say things like dat again? You ever gonna run off from me again? What da ya have ta say to yor mama now? Huh? Huh?"

"Mama! Please stop! I love you, Mama. I won't ever do that again, just please stop! I love you!"

When she was completely worn out, she stopped. She started circling me like an animal about to eat her prey. I was wondering if she might start in on me again. I just laid there, begging for forgiveness, looking up at her. She was totally out of breath. I could hardly breathe myself through all the screaming and crying. I was a bloody mess. I had cried until I could cry no more. Only a breath of a whimper was left, begging Mama to stop and promising to never sass her again. I just laid there with my clothes half torn off. My body was lying on the carport floor, wrapped around the pole, still tied, looking up at her, begging for mercy for her to stop. She finally did.

She left me lying there, whimpering and licking my cuts and bruises. I was wondering just what I had done that was so bad to cause my mama to hate me so much? How could she hate me so much that she would do this to me? How could a mama get so mad and go into a frenzy as if she were in a mad dogfight? What had I done to cause her to beat me so unmercifully? Again, I wanted to run away, but where could I go?

Fred's whippings were more frequent but less severe. He seemed to enjoy giving them to me often. Mama's beatings were less frequent, but I can't tell you how critical they were! It was as if a demon had taken control of her! When she would start into her rant, she just could not control herself! When she would finally stop, I needed medical attention, which I never received. It was never reported to anyone.

This was one of the first cases of severe physical child abuse that I endured. I had gotten whippings before, but not like this one. Usually, Mama gave quick unsuspecting slaps to the face. And I do mean they hurt! In those days, that was the way things were done. Parents could discipline their children in any fashion that they chose, and no one would say a word.

Despite the physical abuse to me, I survived it. Somehow, I still dearly loved my mama. I desperately wanted her to love me back and say those three little words, "I love you." She never did. She was all I had in my life to look up to.

Ana and Ginger by the carport
where Ana was tied up and beaten.

Going back to the day that Mama tied me up and beat me with that limb, I don't remember what I was doing that had me so preoccupied. I didn't want to stop and go check on my little baby brother, Junior. I was probably playing hopscotch on the concrete floor of the carport. I did that a lot. Whatever it was, I should never have made that immature comment about him. I certainly did not mean it. Keep in mind, I was barely nine years old myself. I dearly loved all my little siblings. Junior was so cute and precious! He was mine and Mary's first baby doll. He still let us dress him up, even though now, at this time, we had Ginger as our new baby to play with. Junior was the only boy. He didn't know it; because he was living with three girls, so he thought he was a girl, I guess. He had a right to think he was a girl at the time because we dressed him in our dresses! We all played together as four little girls. I was the oldest, so I was the boss. When I wasn't around, Mary was next in charge. However, she wasn't as bossy as I was. Junior minded her anyway because she was the boss in charge. Mary and I knew that Junior was the favorite child because he was the only boy of Mama and Fred's. Fred doted over him. When Fred was at home, Junior was always on his lap. Fred was never sweet and loving to the rest of us. I had to be very careful not to make Junior cry while around Fred, for fear of Fred's dreadful backhand across my face. By the way, before Fred came home from work, the dresses came off Junior! He was once again a little boy.

One night, I was changing the diaper on Ginger. I loved my baby sister, and I loved to make her laugh. After cleaning her up, before putting back on her diaper, I started blowing on her fat little belly with my mouth and making a funny noise. She was really laughing because it was tickling her belly, at her belly button. Fred came into the room and said, "What are you doing?" As a child, I had no idea what he thought I was doing wrong, but it must have been something terrible! I believe he must have been judging me by what he might have done.

He hauled off and gave me a full-faced-slap so hard that I literally saw stars as I fell to the floor. Everything blacked out except red, white, and blue lights, dancing around in my head. Literally! I do not know how long I was on the floor, but when I woke up, I had a terrible headache. The baby was no longer in the room, and neither was Fred.

I guess his evil mind was at work, thinking I was hurting the baby or something, even though the baby was laughing. Whatever his sick mind was thinking, I paid for it again! Mama said and did nothing as usual. That night I cried myself to sleep. I rolled off the bed toward the wall to hide. I was hoping someone would wake up the next morning and see I wasn't there and miss me. They didn't.

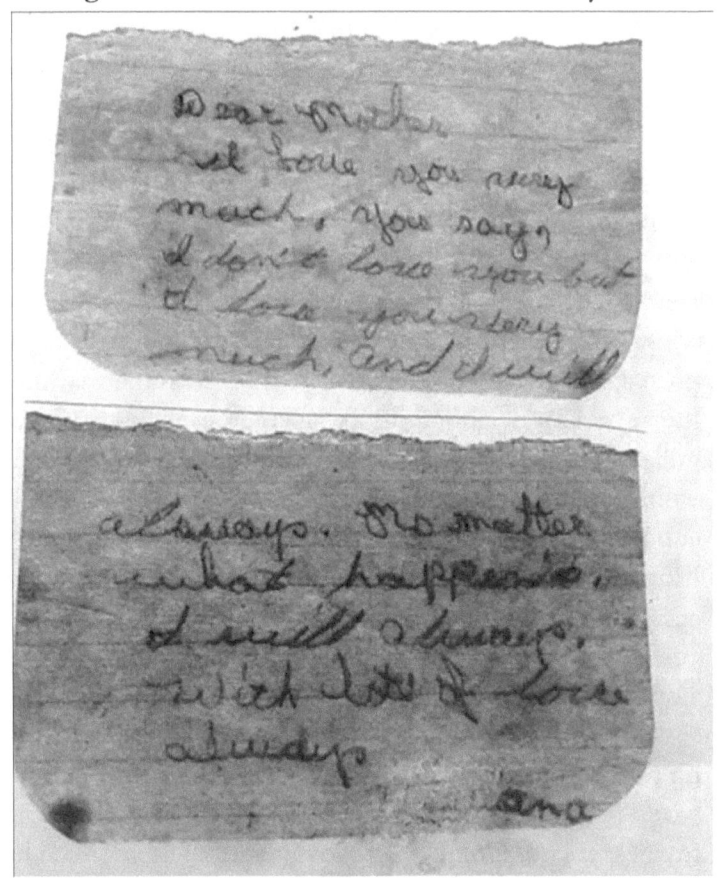

Note from Ana to Mama, kept from years long ago.

The next time Fred was nice to me was very much like the first time. "Come sit on my lap."

With slow hand moves up my leg, he said, "I'm tired, let's take a nap."

I have no idea where Mama was. I ended up in his bed. The next unsuspecting move on his parts was when he pulled out his penis. I had never seen anything that ugly in my life! I had seen my baby brother's penis before, but this thing was big, ugly, and smelled bad! "Hold it for me," he said.

In his drunken stupor, he rolled over and vomited on the side of the bed . . . I got the hell out of there.

Same song, another stanza!

Did I tell Mama this time? No! I didn't want another whipping from Fred! Just like the time when I wrote that letter to Robby pleading for him to come to rescue me from Fred. Then Mama showed that letter to Fred, and he whipped me. I was afraid that Mama would not believe me once again. After all, she didn't believe Ellen that day, nor the next-door neighbor girl. How could I tell her that Fred pulled out his tally whacker and told me to hold it? Mama would only see things through Fred's lies. "He was drunk, and he certainly didn't remember doing such a thing. I must have made it up." I can just hear her response to my accusations.

Just keep quiet, and it will go away . . . so I thought and hoped.

One summer day, after third grade had ended, I woke up to find that one of the most heartbreaking things in the world had happened to me. The next-door neighbors with my best friend, Donna, had moved away during the night. I was so sad. I cried and cried. I was not allowed the opportunity to say good-bye to my one and only dear friend. I wasn't allowed to talk to her at home anymore because of that deplorable incident with Fred. We could only talk at school. We really did not know why we were no longer allowed to visit in her home. Now that school was out, we could no longer visit anywhere. There was a chain-link fence that ran between our yards. Under the fence was a gap between the fence and the ground. The day the family moved, I found that conch shell that I loved so much stuffed into that gap. It was left behind by my friend and her family for me; they knew how much I loved it. At first, I did not understand why the shell was there. Mama told me that they left it there for me, and they wanted me to have it. A little piece of friendship was left behind for me when I needed a friend so badly.

I still think of that dear, caring family today, and the kindness they showed to a poor white trash, little girl who lived next door to them on Navajo Road in 1959-60. That family will never know what their kindness meant to me back then when I desperately needed their friendship and goodness in my dark little life.

After my dear friend moved away, I found another friend who lived across and down the street. I do not remember her name, but I do remember that she lived with her grandparents, and she had polio. I would go and visit with her whenever I could slip off. Mama would not willingly let me leave the yard anymore. This little girl could only watch television from her wheelchair. She was always so happy when I would come to visit. I felt so sorry for her. Her grandparents seemed happy when I would come over to visit and break up her long boring day. It doesn't matter how bad you have it, there is always someone else who has it worse. I was so thankful that I did not have her condition. I tried to be cheerful to her and make her laugh when I was around. I wanted her to have a bright spot in her otherwise dull little life. She did not go to school as far as I knew. She also had trouble talking. She liked me, and I liked her. We enjoyed watching cartoons together. It was a simple friendship, made of nothing but caring for one another and expecting nothing in return. All our friendships should be like this.

Just beyond the plum trees on the right side of our house was a drainage ditch that separated us from the other next-door neighbors, whom we never met. One day, I was playing on top of the drainage ditch mound. I had successfully and slowly pulled all the legs off an Indian grasshopper and played with it until it was dead. Sorrowfully, I then proceeded to give it a proper Christian burial. The burial was complete with a toothpick cross and full prayers. I had buried and unburied the grasshopper five or six times before I heard a noise. Something was splashing in the water below me. I looked down and *lo and behold!*

"Lo and behold," this phrase was used frequently in our family. I do not know for sure, but I think it means: Get ready! Humble yourself! I'm about to tell you something extraordinary!

So, I looked down, and lo and behold! It was a cottonmouth moccasin trying to get up the mound. I ran in and told Mama about it. Do you think she believed me? No! I had to tell her several times and beg her to come quickly and see. After she realized I was serious and scared, she got a hoe and came with me. She tried to kill it, but she was only able to chase it off

Was Mama so preoccupied with other things that she didn't want to be bothered by my childish chatter? Why didn't she listen to me? Why didn't she take me seriously the first time? What else would she not take me seriously about in the future?

Theo, Tooty, and Teddy were still living with Fob. He had to keep them; after all, Mama had abandoned them. Fob had no choice but to keep them. At that time, Opee had moved out and had joined the Marines. Occasionally, the three older children came to visit us on weekends.

I was always jealous of my sister Tooty because she was twelve years old, I was only nine. She seemed so grown up. I wanted to be grown up so badly. I thought she was smarter than me. Tooty was visiting with us on one of those weekends when she started her menstruation cycle. I had no idea why Mama was spending so much time with Tooty in private, but I didn't like it one little bit! Since Tooty was older than me, she always got the Little Miss Pixy set for Christmas; I wanted one too! I never got one. Usually, at Christmas, we only got one gift. The Little Miss Pixie set was a set of perfume, lotion, and powder for a little girl to primp with and pretend to be all grown up. I wanted to primp and be grown up more than Tooty did, so why didn't I get it for Christmas? Tooty never appreciated it anyway! Now she had a big secret, and I wanted to know what it was! Mama was showing her more attention than she ever showed to me. Maybe Mama loved her more than me, I thought. I was sure she did!
However, Mama never said, "I love you," to Tooty either.

I finally got it out of Tooty. Mama had torn up old baby diapers to use as pads for Tooty. It was a bloody mess when I saw what was going on. Still, I thought that was such a grown-up thing. I wanted to do it too. Tooty had big breasts. I wanted big breasts too. Whatever she was doing, I wanted to do. It just wasn't fair that she was ahead of me in everything.

One day, I decided I would take matters into my own hands. I wanted breasts, and it hadn't happened yet, so I made it happen. In our carport, we had a big sack of small red potatoes, which Mama had bought from the Farmer's Market. I took a strip of baby diaper material, tied it around my chest, and stuffed it with two small potatoes. *Voila!* Instant success! No one would notice, right? Wrong! I was the laughingstock of the family! To this day, my sister reminds me of my little taters.

10.
Hell on Navajo Road / Fourth-Grade

It is not my intention to make this little book pornographic; therefore, no details will be given as to the molestation. That would be conjuring up the devil! Besides, most of which I have lived through, gotten past, and moved on. The memories of such are only dim, dark, bad nightmares that I do not wish to live through again.

Summertime was for going to the farmer's market and buying peas, butterbeans, okra, corn, and tomatoes. On Saturday afternoons, we would all sit around in a circle, spread newspapers in the middle of the floor, and shell the peas and beans. It seemed like an endless ordeal! After the work was done, Mama would make tomato sandwiches for all of us to enjoy, then we would watch our usual Saturday night westerns. Later, for us night owls, we would watch Wrestling Live on Channel Five, or maybe late-night horror movies.

Fred never helped with shelling of the peas and beans; he always got drunk. If it was Saturday, it was his time to get drunk, that was just the way it was! He would drink a full bottle of Four Roses whiskey, straight! Maybe he would drink two bottles or more. Then he would roll his eyes around and get obnoxious. Sometimes, he would try to sing. Usually, he would fall asleep and pee on himself. Woe be unto me if Mama wasn't around, for I knew what would ensue! He would jet his eyes at me. I would look away. He would keep this up until he would catch me looking back at him. Then he would shoot his eyes toward his bedroom.

He was talking to me with his eyes again. I hated him for doing this.

On this particular night, when his "foreplay" started, I scurried across the floor toward Mary and cuddled up with her. I peeked back to see his response. He squinted his bloodshot eyes at me and mouthed out something like, "You little . . ." then he reared back his hand as if he was going to backslap me. I immediately looked away again. I never looked back again that night. He went to bed alone. Whew! I got out of that one! The next day, he said nothing, as if he didn't remember. I was glad!

It was time for school to start again in 1960. This year, we were rerouted to a downtown school, Oakdale Elementary School. Mary and I had to ride another great big yellow school bus. I was now in fourth grade, and Mary was entering the first grade. As usual, I had the opportunity for a fresh start at a new school. My dear friend Donna had moved away so I had to make another new friend, which would not be easy for me, but I would try.

Mary and I sat together on the school bus every day. It seemed like a long way to the new school. After we arrived, it was disappointing to see our new school building was old and rundown looking. On top of that, it was also frustrating to know that I had gotten an old rundown teacher! Mrs. McLeod was not the least bit lenient to poor, untidy little girls from my neck of the woods, but I learned to cope with her. It was near the first of the school year, and we were studying Alaska. My friend Donna had lived in Alaska with her family before moving to Alabama. I had heard her family talk about living there, so I thought I knew a little about that state. I really wanted to fit in and contribute to the class, so I raised my hand. The teacher called on me. I lied and said that I used to live in Alaska. The teacher said, "Oh! Tell us what it was like!"

I had no idea what to say after that. I did not expect that I would have to expound on the subject, so I just made up something that I thought it would be like.

I said, "Well, we lived in an igloo. I had a friend that lived next door to us, and I would go visit with her. Her mother would give us milk and cookies." There was a strange silence from Mrs. McLeod as she stared at me. Of course, she knew that was a lie! She just said,
"Okay, thank you."

That was the end of that! What a great start to a new school year! She never liked me much after that, I thought. Maybe I just felt guilty because I knew she saw through my lie.

You see, I desperately wanted to be like the other little girls who were from decent families. That day in fourth grade, I was trying to vicariously live my life through the life of my friend Donna. I failed miserably. I just didn't have what it took to be from a good, decent family. However, I knew in my heart of hearts that I would have it all one day!

Sometimes, Mama would send me walking to the country store about half a mile down the road. There were all sorts of pretty wildflowers along the roadside. Walking to and from, I always picked a bouquet of those lovely wildflowers for my mama. I don't remember her ever putting them in water, but I loved her anyway. (That was just a random thought...)

Thanksgiving came around that year. Our little white house was full of relatives whom I loved and had not seen in quite some time. I was especially glad to see my buddy, best friend, little playmate, and big brother Teddy.

Fred hated Teddy, for Teddy reminded him of Fob. Just as I was, Teddy was a stepchild. Fred would hit Teddy up beside the head with his fist and say, "You little Fob Waterman!" Teddy could do nothing about it, being only ten years old and frail himself. He dared not tell Fob about how Fred mistreated him on those rare visits, for Fob would have come over and killed Fred for sure! Or at least, Fob would forbidden Teddy from visiting with us had he known how Fred mistreated him. Yes! Teddy and I paid the price for being Fred's stepchildren. We both hated him. It seems he was always hellbent on finding new reasons to slap us both around. Mama would just watch and say nothing.

P.S. Years later in life, Teddy went to visit Ellen. Ellen was on the telephone with Fred. When Teddy entered her home, Ellen said, "Teddy, I'm talking with Fred, do you want to speak with him?" Teddy responded, "Who? Fred Oder? No, I don't have anything to say to that S.O.B.! Tell Fred Oder that I weigh 250 pounds, and if he wants to hit me up beside my head with his fist now, like he did when I was a kid, tell him to come on. I can take it now; but he won't like my reaction!"

Now, back to the Thanksgiving story. . . On this particular Thanksgiving Day, our one and only bathroom was occupied for what seemed to be a very long time. Uncle Terry was a big fat man, and it was taking him a very long time to do his business. I had to go, and I had to go right then! So, I did what any self-respecting little girl would do to keep from soiling her one and only pair of good panties----I found a place to go!

I went behind the carport, squatted, and relieved myself. There was just one problem, I didn't have any toilet paper! So, no one would know what I had done, I started covering up the evidence. As I was covering, I noticed that the coconut from the coconut pie was moving . . . in my bowel movement! It wasn't coconut. It was worms! I had worms! I was petrified! What would I do? What *could* I do? This was undoubtedly the end of my life. I ran inside and summoned Mama to come quickly and see. I had discovered my death sentence! Not only was I embarrassed, now I was going to die! Would these things eat me alive from the inside out? How did I get these worms? Probably from eating fish; Mama told me that fish had worms in them! What were we going to do about this horrible, offensive, and frightful situation? I begged Mama to please not tell anyone about this sickly, deadly infestation of man-eating worms . . . *eeer* little girl-eating worms that I had. At least, do not tell anyone until I was dead and gone. I just don't think I could have stood up to the embarrassment of it all! I can just hear the talk now. "Ana not only looks wormy, but she has 'em too! Don't touch her . . . you might catch 'em!"

As far as I know, she told no one. I guess she was embarrassed also to find out that I had worms. A simple little red pill for a week took care of the squiggles. I was relieved to learn that I wasn't going to die!

It was time for the Spring Festival at Oakdale Elementary School in 1961. The theme was "Colonial Days." All the girls in my class wore the same style of dress. My dress was lavender taffeta, trimmed in black ribbon with white lace horizontal designs on the front. The dress was floor-length and had leg-of-mutton sleeves. At the time, I had no idea what leg-of-mutton meant, but I thought the sleeves were pretty anyway. All but one other little girl and I had a boy partner; we had to dance with one another. With a name like Ana Oder, who would want to dance with me? So, you can see why I was the last girl to be chosen. I was lucky there was another girl to dance with! Otherwise, I guess I would have been the *featured solo dancer*! I was also lucky that Mama could sew, and she would let me perform at the Spring Festival. I can still remember dancing around in a circle with our little hands high in the air, counting:

> *One two three, point your toe.*
> *One two three, point your toe.*
> *One two three, point your toe.*
> *One two three, and bow.*

Then repeat the same until the music ended. It seemed that the music ended much too soon that night. I loved dancing around in that beautiful lavender dress, even if I was dancing with a girl.

Once again, Mama did not come to see me perform. I wonder if she was just plain worn out from having ten children. She had a hard life, all her days while growing up on a farm, picking cotton in rural Mississippi. Her father beat her also. Then she was forced into marrying Fob at age fifteen, now married to filthy Fred. Maybe she wouldn't come to see me because she was ashamed of the way she looked, because her clothes weren't too nice either. Albeit, I think she just didn't care anymore about much of anything. I think she had about given up on life. She never showed she was proud of me. I desperately needed her to be proud of me. She never showed it and never said: "I love you." But I loved her anyway.

Oh, well! I played with that little lavender dress for another year after that, until I outgrew it. I loved it. I remember washing it and hanging it out on the rusty clothesline. It never got ironed. It eventually had so many holes and rust stains on it from the clothesline; we threw it away. It was never again as pretty as it was on that first night—when I danced in it . . . with another girl.

11.
Hell on Hale Street

It was a bright, sunny day on June 30, 1961. It was my tenth birthday. However, we weren't having a sweet little birthday party for me. Instead, we were packing up to move away from Navajo Road. I hated to leave mine and Mary's most treasured green glider. It wasn't ours anyway; it just came with the house that we rented for a short while. We surely enjoyed it to the fullest! That rusty, green glider was probably the brightest spot that I remember while living there, with sweet little Mary . . . just gliding away . . . without a care in the world . . . most days. (It was the nights and weekends that I had to worry about.)

We had to move away from our home on Navajo Road because the landlord had received word that Fred tried to rape the next-door neighbor's daughter. He didn't want the same thing to happen again, so he conjured up an excuse that he needed our house for his son to live in. What was strange about his story was that the house next door, which he also owned, was vacant. That was the house my friend Donna and her family had lived in. Several months prior, they moved away in the middle of the night to get away from us. It didn't matter, the landlord still wanted us white trash out of his house, so we had to move. I hated to leave. It seemed that this house was the nicest we had ever lived in. It was cool, and we had it all to ourselves. No other family shared the other side.

Well, we packed up everything we owned and left that nice little white house with the cool shade trees and yummy plum trees. God only knows how much I hated to leave that green, rusty metal glider that Mary and I cherished so! We moved to the Little Cities of Alabama, a low-income housing project. We moved into a green slate-sided duplex with absolutely no trees anywhere to be seen throughout the whole project complex. It was a scorching place to live, especially in the summertime. The only thing that we had to keep us cool was one window fan that blew outward. It would suck the air out and pull air back into the apartment through the partially opened windows. It didn't do too good of a job, but it was all that we had, and we were glad to have it.

In the daytime, Mama banished us children to play outside all day. There was no shade, so most of the time, we played under the duplex in the dirt. The duplex was up on cinder blocks, so there was plenty of room for us to sit and dig in the dirt with our spoons. Some of the other kids from the project had a few toys, and they would bring their toy trucks or dolls over. We would play all day in that dirty hellhole of a place we now called our new home.

There was a new game that we learned to play. Someone found a big one-inch-by-twelve-inch board that was about eight feet long. We were industrious little snots, so we made use of this scarce and valuable article of fun. We added a cinder block and . . . *Voila!* We had made a jump-board!

Here's how it worked: One kid gets on one end and another kid on the other, sort of like a seesaw, only you are standing. One kid jumps hard on one end of the board, and it sends the other kid soaring high into the air! When that kid comes back down, he/she jumps hard, down upon the board and sends the other kid high into the air. Then the game continues . . . on and on, on and on. It was great fun. That game was all we had to do that was really fun and exciting. And it was on my side of the tiny yard, where the window fan blew outward. We were cooled by the fan, and we were also "cool," so we thought. It was all fun and games until someone got hurt. Wouldn't you know it, I was the one who got hurt! I fell off one day and sprang my ankle. Mama came out and forbid us to play that game again. I was heartbroken! After all, she had hurt me much worse than that before, during her beatings! So why would she take away all our fun? After Mama put a stop to our jump-boarding, my friends had no reason to come around anymore. It's funny how people can be like that sometimes.

It was sad when someone dragged my board and cinder block off during the middle of the night and started playing with it in their yard on another street. I was never allowed to leave my yard, so I never got to play that game again.

It wasn't long until I started fifth grade. Mary was in second grade. This was my fifth time to go to another new school. Again, I had another chance to have a fresh start. We had to walk to school, along with the other kids on our street. It was less than a mile, I guess, but in the winter months, it seemed longer and especially on rainy days. I don't remember too much about fifth grade, only that I was behind on my multiplication tables. That made me behind in division. Mama never helped me with my homework. I wasn't encouraged to be a good student. I did, however, get whippings for making failing grades . . . I wonder why?

Christmas 1961 was approaching. Little did we know this would be the last Christmas we would spend with Mama. Fred was making decent money, working on the docks of a trucking company; however, he drank it up, and Mama did not know how to manage money. Consequently, we were still living in poverty.

It has been said that *poverty is a state of mind*. I strongly concur. There was no reason why we should have been living poorly. As a little girl, I knew I would rise above all that filth and degradation and be someone, someday. I had set my mind to becoming a better person than those around me, even way back then. Some people can lose everything they own in life and get it all back. Then again, others can be given everything in life and lose it all quickly. It is simply how you look at life. So where are you today? What do you want to do with your life? Are you going to live as a lowlife, or rise above all that garbage? The choice is up to you to make your own way in life. No one is holding you down . . . only your state of mind and your own willpower to do better! Set your goals high, and someone will be there to help you achieve them.

It was a Saturday morning, and Christmas was approaching. We four little ones went with Mama to the local grocery store. There were all sorts of dolls up high on the wall of the store. Beautiful tall, walking dolls with long eyelashes. Some were dressed like cowgirls and ballerinas. Beautiful bride dolls all dressed in white, just waiting for some little girl to pretend love and marriage. There were baby dolls with baby bottles dressed in pink and blue; their eyes could open and close. There were bright, colorful little toy trains rolling around in circles with their smokestacks steaming into the air. Red and blue boys' and girls' bicycles were the best and biggest prize on the wall. Oh, how I wanted one of those beautiful big bicycles! I just knew that Santa would bring me one if I begged my mama diligently enough.

This Christmas, we didn't have a Christmas tree, as we had the year before on Navajo Road. So, I, the industrious one, took it upon myself, as I had done before; set out to find a Christmas tree and decorate it. I went into a vacant lot on the way home from school and spied a straggly little sort of spruce pine bush. The next afternoon, when Mama was unaware, I slipped a butcher knife from the kitchen, went back to that vacant lot and hacked it down. I dragged it home, leaned it on the corner wall, and proceeded to decorate it. Toilet paper made pretty snowflakes. Aluminum foil made excellent stars and icicles. Mary and I used our crayons to draw and color ornaments, then we stuck them in the tree. It was a beautiful tree. Surprisingly, Mama let us keep it.

On Christmas Day, I just couldn't wait to see what Santa had brought to us. Ginger got a baby doll, but not the pretty one that was high on the wall at the grocery store. Mary also got a doll. I was glad that I got the cowgirl walking doll. However, I was disappointed to see that the favorite one, the only boy, my baby brother, Junior, got the beautiful shiny red bicycle! It was my dream to get a bicycle! I was older, and I felt that I deserved it. But he was Fred's son and Fred paid the bills. So, he got it, complete with training wheels. I did get to ride it, sometimes, but only when Fred was not around. He would have beat me for sure had he known that I rode it.

Looking back over the past Christmases, this was one of the best in terms of gifts that we received. I guess it was because Fred made enough money to afford us a few gifts. I honestly was thankful for the gifts. I did feel that I was a little too old for a doll, but I never let on. Mama would have whipped me for sure. I just made sure that Mary got to play with it and enjoy it. I kept my eye on that shiny red bicycle, even though it was too little for me to ride, I still rode it whenever I could.

It was a Saturday afternoon, and Mama and Fred had planned a fishing trip. We children were to stay home with Opee watching over us. Mama gave me two whole dollars and told me I could go to the store and buy some ice cream for us to enjoy while they were away fishing. I was ecstatic! I almost set a record-time-run to the little store to get that ice cream. When I got to the store, I looked over the ice cream, and I was trying to decide what the best buy was for my money. I decided that ice cream wasn't the answer. Instead of buying ice cream, I bought candy instead. I could buy four pieces of taffy for one cent. That meant that I could get four times two hundred equals eight hundred pieces of candy, less the tax. So that was my decision. I returned home with my big purchase. We unwrapped the nearly eight hundred pieces of taffy and wadded them into one big ball. We proceeded to pull the taffy and eat on it all night. We were happy that the candy lasted much longer than the ice cream would have lasted. It was a long, happy night---happy that is until Mama came home and saw my purchase was not what she ordered. Again, another whipping from that razor strap. It was a long and hard beating too. I never knew why she was so mad. . . or why she beat me so badly. If she wanted to do something good for us, why did she get so mad when we enjoyed something good? The taffy was as good as the ice cream, except, it lasted longer than the ice cream. I could see no wrong in what I had done.

Much later in our lives, and just before her death, Mary told me about the one and only time she ever got a whipping from Mama. It happened this way:

Mary was around seven years of age. We were living in the duplex. Us girls always had to wash the dishes. That night, it was Mary's turn.

Mama came in and said, "Now, Mary, when you wash those dishes, I want you to use some elbow grease!"

Mary, not knowing what in this world "elbow grease" was, started looking around the kitchen for some. Ahhh! There it must be! She found a jar of bacon drippings on the stove. She commenced to climb up on the number 2 washtub (that was turned upside down to stand on). She poured the bacon drippings into the wash water and started to wash the dishes. Needless to say, the dishes didn't get clean.

Mary got a whipping! At the time, she never knew why.

That's the way it was, no lesson learned. You know, like: "Here, sweetie, this is what I meant." No, just an ass whipping for having done the wrong thing. Sweet little Mary never did anything intentionally wrong. Mama never did have good judgment when it came to child discipline. Poor ignorant Mama!

Next door to us in that little duplex, there lived a family who had no mother nor father living with them. Four brothers and sisters lived there alone, two of which were older teenagers. They all had fire engine red hair. The oldest big brother worked to pay the bills; he was around eighteen. One little girl was my age, her other brother was around twelve. The oldest teenage girl was sixteen; she had a small bastard child of her own. She was pregnant again with another. She did not want, nor need another illegitimate child. The girl confided in Mama she thought she was around four months pregnant again. She didn't know what she was going to do. Mama's mind started to work, contriving a plan. Mama knew a married couple, who could not have children, but they desperately wanted them. The man and his wife were both terribly overweight;

therefore, the woman could not conceive. Mama devised a plan to help both families out of their unfortunate situations. It happened this way:

Mama introduced the red-headed pregnant girl to the desperate couple. The man decided to divorce his wife and marry the girl according to the contrived plan. The young girl and her bastard child moved in with the man and his newly-divorced-wife. The couple took care of the girl and her child. This was to ensure the girl received proper prenatal care for a healthy delivery.

After about five months, the time came for the delivery. She delivered another healthy baby boy with fire engine red hair. On the birth certificate, the baby boy received the same last name as the man.

When she came home from the hospital, the girl moved out and left the new baby with his new family. The girl and the man later divorced, and the man remarried his original wife. The man and woman now had their desired baby, and the girl got rid of her unwanted baby. They were all happy. It worked out well for all concerned. The young girl received $500 in severance pay, so to speak, for her time and trouble.

"And they lived happily ever after . . ." or so we can only hope. No one ever asked who the father was, or where he was. We can only hope, for the sake of that desperate couple, that the father wasn't her brother!

It was around this time in my life that I started having problems with my stomach. I had learned to read Fred's eyes by now. I could tell when he was mad at me, or when he was saying something much worse . . . like, "Go to the bedroom."

I was in a nervous twit all the time it seems. I tried not to ever look him in the eye, for fear of what I might see. It was never a good thing. It appeared that suppertime was his favorite time to intimidate me. We could be sitting around the dinner table; nothing would be going wrong. Maybe I might say any ole thing . . . and then, there I would get that hateful, disdaining glare from him! I knew he hated me, and he wanted me to shut up. I wished I had never opened my mouth to talk. If that wasn't enough, I would usually get so upset, it would make me throw up right then and there onto my plate and start crying. Then I would have to leave the table without finishing my dinner. (Of course, this didn't make it any too pleasing for the rest of the family, having to witness me vomiting up my butter beans, okra, cornbread, and tomatoes onto my plate.)

Opee would say, "There goes Nibbles puking again."

(He always called me *Nibbles* and *Doorknob Knees*.) I hated it when he called me those names.

No one ever knew what was making me nervous at the table. Mama never asked what the matter was, nor did she care, I guess. Only Fred knew what he was doing to me with his eyes. It was an automatic reaction to his mean looks . . . I would get nervous and throw up. Mean looks were better than his slaps at the table, however. I hated him!

Funny thing, when I finally got away from him, a few years later, all that throwing up stopped.

You know, what adult child molesters don't realize is this:

The things that they are doing to that child . . . they *think* they are getting away with it. And they may be getting away with it. . . for a while. The child may be silent for the time at hand, out of fear, or some other reason, but those things that are happening to her are being recorded indelibly in her brain and psyche for the rest of her life. She will remember them forever, for they are troubling to her. One day, she will be all grown up, and she will be able to stand up for herself and avenge the wrong that has happened to her. One day, the molester may have to come face to face with his past wrongdoings when she brings it all out. She never forgets those tragedies. If she has a forgiving spirit, she might forgive, but she never forgets. Some little girls grow up and get even, or better yet, get revenge. Those nasty ole men have no idea what they are messing with when they molest, bully, run over, and take advantage of little girls! Woe be unto the man who faces the grown-up little girl like me!

There is no statute of limitations on revenge!

12.
Will the Hell Ever Come to an End?

It was a cold rainy night in February 1962. We were still living in that tiny duplex at the Little Cities of Alabama, a low-income apartment complex. Mama was frying chicken. She had to leave and go pick up Fred from work; she left me in charge of the chicken. She told me to take it out of the grease when it was done and turn off the gas burner. That was a big responsibility for a ten-year-old little girl with a short attention span.

A few moments prior, Mama had told me I could take baton lessons so I could be a little majorette. That meant the next year, I could march in the Mardi Gras parade. I am sure it was just a lie that she told me, to put me off from my continual begging. I was so excited! I just had to run and tell the wonderful news to my little red-headed friend, who lived next door. Of course, I overstayed my visit. The chicken was burning. My brother, Opee, came home from work, took the chicken off the stove and saved the duplex from burning down. In a little while, Mama and Fred came home; then I returned home.

Get prepared for me to tell you what happened to me next.

I no sooner stepped in the back door of that little duplex when Mama grabbed me and slammed me against the wall then showed me the black, crispy burned chicken. My eyes widened, and my heart began to pound out of my body!

Mama grabbed the razor strap, which always hung by a nail on the kitchen wall and started beating me unmercifully! I do not know how long the beating lasted, but it seemed like several minutes. She was screaming louder than I was. "Why didn't ya stay here and watch the chicken? Didn't I tell you ta watch dat chicken? Why did ya leave? Are ya ever goin' do dat again? Huh? Huh? What do you have ta say about burnin' the chicken? Huh? Huh? Are you ever gonna do dat again? Huh? Huh?" Over and over . . . it was endless as the blows just kept on pounding down on my back and legs, sometimes hitting me in other more tender places like my genitalia.

I was begging and pleading for her to stop. "Mama, please stop! Mama, I love you. Please, Mama, stop. I love you, Mama. I won't ever do that again. I promise, Mama! I love you!" That was all I could say repeatedly. Until I could say or scream it no more.

She just kept on and on and on. I was flinging around and flouncing around the room, gasping for air, begging her to please stop, but she wouldn't stop. It seemed the more she pounded that razor strap on me, the more of a beating frenzy she went into. She was out of control. It was an out-of-body experience for her. The devil had taken control of her! I was the object of her revenge. Finally, she had worn herself completely out and had to stop. I was limp from the exertion of trying to get away from her. I was cowering on the floor in the corner as I was looking up at her, wondering if she was only taking a break and would start on me again. Her eyes were bloodshot red and wide open with rage. She had lost her eyeglasses from all the confusion. She was puffing and gasping for air as she looked for her glasses and then she walked off. At that moment, I hated her! I already had black and blue whelps and bruises all over my legs, butt, and back. I remember crying so hard that I was whimpering and gasping all night, choking and swallowing snot. I wanted to run away. However, I could hardly walk, much less run anywhere.

I am sure this beating gave Fred much pleasure, to see me get what I deserved for burning his dinner. I could not understand why Mama would beat me so hard if she loved me. The punishment was one thing, even light whippings, I agree with, but the severe beatings that I received were uncalled for. I could barely walk for days. My little skinny legs had half-inch black whelps on my calves for a very long time. I limped around for several days.

This sort of thing would not be allowed to happen today. It is called child abuse in the most real sense of those two words. Mama had that razor strap for one purpose and one purpose only—to whip her children with. However, Fred's three children never got whippings with that razor strap. It was only I who got the bitter end of it. I guess Mama gave me as a sacrifice in order to keep Fred happy. After all, he didn't want me when Mama showed up with Mary and me back in 1955, walking up that dusty red clay hill. He only wanted Mama and Mary, his own blood daughter. I was extra baggage. I had to toe the line and believe me; I dearly paid the price for being Fred's stepdaughter!

I know God knows that I hated Fred. How can I ask for forgiveness for something that I am not sorry for? . . . for hating Fred. God knows that I hated him, but more importantly, he (God) knows why I hated him. I think God can forgive me for the sin of hatred. Fred is the one who must fear God, not me. I am a child of God. God is my real Father, and I love him.

Again, another holiday came around. It was Easter 1962. No Easter bunny was to be seen anywhere around our little duplex. The two youngest ones had no idea what day it was, but Mary and I did. At school, we had made decorations of Easter eggs and bunnies, chicks, and the likes. So, I was well aware that this was the day when there should be Easter baskets and candy found when we awakened. This year, Mama did not even bother to make us a new outfit to wear.

It was just an ordinary Sunday morning. We never went to church. Fred was recovering from his usual Saturday night drunkenness. Crackers and tomato juice were his hangover remedy. He sat at the breakfast table, blurry eyed and stinking to high heavens! I dared not speak to him for fear of his backhand across my face. I knew not to ask why we didn't get anything from the Easter bunny. I pretended not to know what day it was, Mary did the same. Although we both knew, we only whispered about it quietly while we were alone.

Later that day, our oldest sister Ellen came over, and we all went for a ride. I asked her for a quarter, and if would she stop and let me go into a convenient store. She gave me the quarter, and I went in. I purchased twenty-four pieces of Mary Janes. (Mary Janes were four pieces of taffy for one cent all in one pack.) So, one quarter would buy: twenty-four packs of Mary Janes, times four in each pack, equals ninety-six pieces of candy---total, plus the one cent tax. I asked the clerk if I might have four little brown paper bags also. He gave them to me. I came back to the car, smiling, but I said nothing.

When we got home, I went straight into the bathroom with my secret package. I tore the four little brown bags into little brown baskets. I shredded toilet paper and stuffed it into the four little baskets to make it look like grass. I unpackaged the twenty-four packs of Mary Janes and put the loose pieces into each basket for our Easter candy. Each of us four kids got twenty-four pieces of candy in a little brown basket.

To keep from divulging the secret, without anyone noticing, I hid the little brown paper baskets behind the couch. A few minutes later, I asked Mary to look behind the couch for my jacks' ball, (which wasn't there.) She found the baskets! Oh! What a surprise! The Easter bunny really did come! He must have hidden our surprises! Everyone's sadness turned to joy.

Isn't it amazing how a very small thing can do so much good? A simple twenty-four cents for four little children. Even before Mama died, I was their little mama and didn't know it. I had no idea what was about to happen in a few short months that would change our lives so drastically.

My brother Opee had recently returned home from serving his duty in the Marines. He had his own private bedroom in our small duplex. In his room, he had a large reel-to-reel tape recorder. He loved music and would tape songs from the radio for his future enjoyment. One song in particular I remember that was popular back then was:

Splish-Splash

by Bobby Darin.

It goes like this:

> Splish-Splash, I was takin' a bath
> Long about a Saturday night, yeah
> A rub dub, just relaxin' in the tub
> Thinkin' everythin' was alright
> Well, I stepped out of the tub
> I put my feet on the floor

I wrapped the towel around me, and I opened the
door

And then a splish, splash
I jumped back in the bath
Well, how was I to know
There was a party goin' on?
There was a-splishin' and a-splashin'
Movin' and a-groovin'
Rockin' and a-rollin', yeah, yeah
Bing, bang, I saw the whole gang
Dancin' on my living room rug, yeah
(. . . on and on . . . you get the idea . . .)

Being the young little actress that I was, I loved to sing that song. One day, Mama was in Opee's bedroom, sitting on the bed, having a conversation with him. I now had an audience! So, I grabbed my little invisible microphone and jumped into his room. I then proceeded to perform that song for them.

I began to sing, "Splish-Splash, I was takin' a bath," then I struck a cute little pose as if I were bathing under my arms.

I proceeded. . . "Long-about-a-Sat . . ."

Yeah! -----Long-about-a-that-time----I got no farther. It was at that very moment when I felt the sudden hot, blistering, teeth-shattering slap across my left ear--by Mama!

It took me a couple of seconds for the pain to go from my face--to my brain--and back down. At that moment, I realized what had happened to me. I was embarrassed for this to take place in front of Opee because I wanted to impress my big brother with my talents. I am sure my eyes widened with shock, as my mouth flew open wide. I looked up, and my eyes locked with Opee's; then I ran out of his room. I wanted to disappear forever. I crawled underneath the duplex, put my head between my knees, and sobbed my heart out while sitting there in the filthy dirt.

To this day, Opee says he cannot remember what in the hell Mama wanted to talk to him about, that was so important to warrant such treatment to me. I have irreparable nerve damage in both of my ears today. All of us children do. Shame on Mama!

In June of 1962, I was allowed to go to Vacation Bible School at a little Baptist Church nearby our duplex. On Wednesday of that week, the pastor shared with the older children the plan of salvation. He told us how Jesus had come to the earth as a baby. When he was a grown man, God's real purpose for sending him to the earth was to die for our sins in order that we might have eternal life in heaven with him and God the Father. Jesus was the sacrifice for our sins.

I knew what sin was. I felt that guilt when the preacher talked about it. I repented from my sins, which were a heavy burden on me as a child. What I had seen, endured, and been exposed to was wrong and sinful, and I knew it. At the time, I felt all these wrongful things that were happening to me were my fault. I confessed, admitted, and was truly sorrowful for all that I had done. I asked for Jesus's forgiveness in order to go to heaven when I died.

I cried and cried; it was sincere repentance. I can still feel it today. That was the day I asked Jesus to come into my heart. He did, and he is still there today.

That next Friday night was the commencement service for the Vacation Bible School. I had the honor of carrying the Bible into the Church building. I asked Mama to come and see me. This was one of the most important moments in my life and a very big accomplishment for me. She would not come to see me carry that Bible. No one in my family was there to be proud of me. Only Jesus saw me, and I am sure he was proud!

It was around this time that the repulsive encounters of molestation came to an end. I was a changed person. I was no longer that little sacrificial lamb to Fred. I stood up to Fred, and I learned that he would back down. I was bold in my Christian belief, and I wanted to evangelize the world, starting right at home. Fred had a different attitude toward me after that. He almost had a slight respect for me after that. I guess he had the fear of God scared into him. Rightfully so!

Much later in life, I was able to forgive Fred for all the hateful abuse and molestation. He never admitted his transgressions, nor did he ever ask me to forgive him. I just forgave him in order to have peace in my own heart. You see, I figure it this way:

Forgiveness *is not saying, "what you did is okay." It's just letting go.*
Not forgiving *is like taking in poison and hoping it will kill the other person.*

At the end of June 1962, I turned eleven years old.

It was August 19 of that same year that my mama died and was released from her hell here on this earth.

The next night, after we heard the terrible news of her death, we four little ones were taken to the funeral home to see Mama. She was lying there in her casket, which was nothing more than a wooden box covered with blue, velvet cloth. There she was, as I looked at her; I thought she was more beautiful than I had ever seen her before; she looked like an angel. Her hair was fixed by a beautician. It was a Jackie Kennedy hairstyle—bouffant and pulled back on the top with two small curls hanging down on each side of her forehead. She had on a pale pink chiffon ruffled funeral gown. Her hands were folded at her waist, with a slight smile on her little pink lips. I cried as I leaned into the casket and kissed her.

I was told not to kiss her too many times, because it would make the body turn blue. Her body was cold; it surprised me. I hated to let her go. I knew I would never see her again; not after she was lowered into that hole in the ground the next day.

As I was standing there staring into the casket at the corpse of our dead mother, I was holding the little hand of my youngest baby sister, Ginger. Ginger was not yet five years old and still talked baby talk. She looked up at me with tear-filled eyes, and a runny nose, then she asked, "When Mama dona' wate up and tee her pruty plowers?" All I could blurt out was, "She's not…she's dead!" I don't think Ginger understood. I know, I certainly didn't understand *why* she was dead.

So, there we were: two broken-hearted little girls, standing hand-in-hand, staring at the dead body of our mama…wondering what would become of us now? Now that Mama was gone forever.

Her death was as if all hell had broken loose in my life! What I didn't realize was, I had already been living in and through my worse hell. Now, this event, (Mama's death) was the beginning of the end to all that. It was to be that final giant step I had to take in order to cross over to that mountain peak that would ultimately release me from my hell. My life would slowly but surely get better, but it would still be a smoldering hell's fire that I would have to continue and try to put out for a very long time. In order to move on, I had a great deal of baggage to unload and put behind me. However, at the time, while I was staring into her casket, I had no idea what laid ahead of me. Only God knew his ultimate perfect plan for my life. At the time, I was not willing to listen to him. It hurt.

My oldest brother Robby took us four little ones across the street and bought us something to eat. I could not eat without throwing up salty, frothy foam. The paper wrapper that was around my soda straw had the word "Sweetheart" on it. I tore that word off and placed it in my mama's hands when I returned to her casket. Then I went over and sat alone against the wall of the funeral home. I watched as family members and friends came to visit and pay their respects. Some acted civilized, some acted like I expected them to behave, like a Waterman would act---uncouth. Some of the women were flouncing around and crying out loud just for show. I couldn't believe what I was seeing. I just sat there, against the wall, looking around. I was mad---mad at God for what had happened to me.

The next day was never-ending. The funeral service was miserable, morose, and sorrowful. Everyone was crying, as two heart-wrenching songs were sung by the preacher's two young daughters.

"No Tears in Heaven" and "I'll Meet You in the Morning" were the two songs the young girls sang in their country, red-neck twang. It was a tear-jerking experience. We were able to sit up front, close to Mama's casket, as if we were the honored guests in some big event. I guess we were. The preacher talked about how he believed my mama received Jesus as her Savior on her deathbed, or shall I say in her iron lung? I wondered about that. After so many years of pain and suffering that she placed on her children, could this be possible? Could Jesus really forgive a corrupt person such as my mama, who purposely did mean and spiteful things all the way up until the day she died?

Six Marines carried Mama's casket to the hearse. The hearse was then driven to the Mississippi graveyard, where Mama was laid to rest beside Baby John.

My heart was pounding with fear when I watched her casket as it was lowered into the ground. It was a sight I will never forget! I was surprised I was allowed to view. I don't think they could have stopped me. My oldest sister Ellen was videotaping the whole thing. It was a gut-wrenching day.

No young child should have to go through the horrors and heartbreak of losing their mother. No matter how mean, cruel, or deplorable that mother may have been to her children, she was still their mother, and they need her for love, guidance, support, and protection. Although I rarely received any of that, I still had hope as long as she was alive. However, when she was dead and gone, all hope of ever obtaining love, guidance, support, and protection *vanished forever.*

She took it all with her.

13.
Released from Hell, Still Smoldering

When Mama died, I know the only reason that Fred didn't send me back to Fob was that he needed me to be the babysitter, which I was and a good one at that! A mean, little bossy big sister. I guess I liked having that authority. Or maybe it was the last command that Mama gave to me, *"You take care of the little ones and don't let them play in the street, 'cause they might get run over and killed. You be their little mama."* I went from being the big sister to becoming the little mama.

I had to grow up very fast when Mama died. There was no one there to take care of us, just me to take care of the three little ones. I must not have done too good a job taking care of them or myself, because we played in the rain at night in the street gutters. I allowed them to play along with me. There was no one to stop us. Consequently, I came down with pneumonia in November of that year, which was only twelve weeks after Mama died. I probably would have died had too it not been for Uncle Terry, Fred's brother, calling to check on us that Thanksgiving Day. On this particular Thanksgiving Day, no one was there, just us four little ones. I don't know where Fred was. Opee was living with us at the time, but he wasn't there either. He was probably visiting his girlfriend's family for the Thanksgiving holiday. So, there was no Thanksgiving dinner for us little ones that year. I fixed sandwich bread with syrup mixed with canned milk for the three younger ones to eat. I was too sick to eat. When Uncle Terry called,

I told him how I felt; I could not breathe. My lungs were hurting. The Oder family came over and got the little ones, and then they took me to the hospital. I stayed there a week. After that, we all moved in with Fred's sister, Aunt Patty and her husband Uncle Arty, along with their three children. This family was very decent, and kind, not at all like Fred, who was the black sheep of the family.

Moving in with this lovely family was as if heaven had opened up for me! I had reached that mountain peak and had crossed over, out of my hell. I had a new life ahead of me, a new beginning. The only difference was, this time, I would not be considered white trash. I had never lived with anyone other than my mother before; this would be a real change for me. I was looking for another mama to love me. Aunt Patty was the one who could fill those shoes.

Aunt Patty was good to me. I never felt that she or Big Mama Oder treated me any differently from the other little ones, who were their real blood grandchildren. As a matter of fact, I sort of think I was treated special, or even better. I was older and smarter than the younger ones. Aunt Patty took a lot of time with me; I never had that kind of attention before. I liked that. Aunt Patty took me to the dentist for the first time in my life. My health started to improve. She taught me proper hygiene; how to brush my teeth, shampoo and roll my hair, manicure my nails, and totally cleanse my body. I wanted to primp and be pretty, and she helped me get started at it. She also corrected a lot of my wrong English words. She taught me to be a little lady.

Aunt Patty had three children of her own: one daughter, Lucy who was three years old, and two boys. My sister, Ginger, was five. Lucy would boss Ginger around. Ginger had no choice but to take it. I was the oldest of the seven kids. Lucy thought I was pretty and looked up to me. They all did.

Every Sunday, we were taken to Eastdale Baptist Church. In January 1963, I was finally allowed to be baptized. I accepted Jesus as my Savior back in June of 1962, but Mama would not permit baptism. (She thought it meant I would be joining the church, and the preacher might be coming around asking for money.) Anyway, Brother Durden was the godly pastor who was bestowed the honors of baptizing me when I was eleven years old. I knew at that time, my hell's fires were finally being extinguished for good…not because the baptismal waters have any mystical powers at putting out fire, or anything like that. But because I knew I was now safely in the hands of a loving God who would see to it that no more harm would come to his child (me). I was in a Christian home where I knew someone truly loved and would care for me.

Aunt Patty treated me like a little princess. She would take us to the church crisis closet and let us pick out any clothes that we wanted. That closet was full of beautiful dresses. We loved getting new things to wear. Even though the clothes were used, they looked new. Also, Big Mama was always making us new things to wear. We certainly needed new, fresh clothing.

There was never a more wonderful childhood Christmas than the Christmas of 1962. It was the first time I learned the true meaning of Christmas. I thought it was all about Santa Claus. I had no idea that it was Jesus' birthday. It was heart touching to hear how God sent his only son to be born of a virgin, and how she wrapped him in swaddling clothes and laid him in a manger. His real purpose for coming to this earth was to grow up and give himself as our sacrifice for our sins, so we could go to heaven and be with him and God the Father. What a great story! The story goes on to tell how angels proclaimed his birth, the shepherds came to worship him on that blessed day. Wise men brought gifts to honor him when he was a child. That is one of the reasons why we give gifts today at Christmas time.

What a magical time it was that Christmas at Aunt Patty's home! I had never seen such a beautifully decorated home! Their home smelled of freshly cooked turkey, dressing, pumpkin pie, and sugar cookies. There was holly garland with flashing lights rolling and folding on and off the mantle of the old upright piano. A carefully placed nativity scene was displayed on the coffee table to remind us of the reason for the season. The big freshly cut fir Christmas tree filled the house with its sweet fragrance. That tree took up almost all the floor space in the living room with hundreds of colorful flashing and bubbling lights. Real glass ornaments covered the tree as well as real peppermint candy canes. A beautiful angel graced the top of the tree. She looked down at me with winking and blinking eyes as if to say, "The good news is here, Jesus is born, and he loves you!" The base of that gorgeous tree was mounded up with shiny foil wrapped presents with big bows and ribbons. There were more gifts than I have ever seen in my life, all waiting for us children to tear into on Christmas Day. Christmas morning arrived and us children could hardly wait to get up and see what were in those gifts! Unlike other years, we received more than just one present. We got more toys and gifts than I had ever received in my whole life combined. I got my very own precious white-bound Bible, a beautiful bride doll, a toy sewing machine, bubble bath, a make-up kit, manicure set, on and on. But it wasn't the gifts that made it so special. It was the love that I saw and felt in that beautiful, loving home. It was the warmth and compassion that was passed on to me, my brother and sisters in our time of sadness and need. Only Christ-like love can exemplify that. Only the love of God can come through with that type of love when others need it so desperately. My newly found Aunt Patty and Uncle Arty gave that Christ-like love to me, my brother and sisters.

Thank you, Aunt Patty, I love you for taking us in, loving and caring for us in our time of need. I will see you again in heaven...I know!

On Easter of that next year in 1963, a lady from the church made all four of our Easter outfits. My dress was yellow. She bought my first pair of "Bra Forms," so the package read. I was so proud of them. I wore them every day for years. I would wash them by hand every week.

We only lived with Aunt Patty and her dear, sweet family from November 1962 until May of 1963. After that time, we four were all put into foster homes. We had to become a ward of the state to be eligible to be placed in the orphanage, where we would soon be going to live. From May until August 1963, we lived in four different foster homes. In August, we three older ones went to live the rest of our childhood at the orphanage. It was one of the best things that could have happened to us. Ginger stayed with Aunt Patty for another year or two. Because she was so young, she was slower arriving at the orphanage. Aunt Patty wanted to "Mother" her as long as possible.

"Even a child is known by his doings." (Prov. 20:11)

Aunt Patty took us by car to the small little town in mid-state Alabama, where the orphanage was located. It seemed to take all day to get there. When we finally arrived, it was late afternoon. We unloaded our brown paper bags of clothing, what dear small amount that we had, and walked up to the big administration building. The superintendent of the orphanage met us and briefly showed us around. Then we were taken to our respective cottages where we were to live. Mary and I were assigned to live in the same cottage while Junior went to the boy's side of the campus.

Aunt Patty went in with Mary and me to check out our new home. The other fifteen girls in the dormitory were curious about their new roommates. In my cottage, there were two dormitories— the big girl's side and little girl's side. Mary and I were assigned to live in the little girl's dormitory. I was glad that we were kept together so I could keep track of Mary.

Aunt Patty wanted to make sure that we made friends at the orphanage, so she told the girls that I could fix hair. Not many girls could do that, so that made me a rare commodity.

After we halfway got settled in, Aunt Patty had to leave; it was a long way to drive back home alone. I cried when she left. I dearly loved my aunt Patty, because she was the one person in my whole life that was truly good and sweet to me. She was the first person who truly took a life-long interest in me. It would be a long time before we would see her again.

After dinner, that night, one of the big girls asked if I would fix her hair. I looked at her long, extremely curly, red hair. How was I to fix her hair? All I knew to do was wash and roll hair up on curlers. I attempted it anyway! She had never had her hair rolled up on curlers before; rolling it on curlers smoothed out some of the kinky curls. The next Sunday morning, I brushed her hair out, and it looked very nice, better than it had ever looked before. From then on, she liked me. Come to find out, she was one of the meanest girls in the house! I had just won her over to my side, and I sure needed that friend!

Going to the orphanage was a huge adjustment for us. Again, I had to step up to the plate and be the big sister. We came from a poor white trash family, but so did some of the other kids there! I had to learn to fight or get my ass kicked. I chose to fight, or better said, standup for myself and for my brother and sister. I was better at bluffing than fighting. I had rather bluff my way out of a fight than to actually do the battle. When I did get into an actual fight, I usually won, because I wouldn't give up! I knew if I did, there would be another bigger kid to take me on the next time. It is always best to be the winner! I had to act meaner than I was because I was little and skinny for my age. However, I was just smart enough to know not to engage in a fight with a bigger girl, one which I would surely lose! It was better to walk away from those fights.

I was insecure. There was no one there on my side, just me against the world, and my brother and sister for me to take care of. The orphanage had social workers that we had to visit regularly. They never asked questions about my past life or about the bad things that had happened to me prior to coming to the orphanage. So, they had no idea about the beatings and the molestation from Fred. The social workers were only concerned about how I was adjusting to living at the orphanage and away from my family. Being taken away from my family was hard, but anything was better than living with Fred! I liked the orphanage, but it had its drawbacks too. Institutional life was hard on us. Living with fifteen other girls was quite an adjustment.

However, I must say we were very fortunate to have had the opportunity to live at that orphanage. We were very well cared for physically, mentally, and spiritually. We always had three warm meals per day. If we needed a new suit of clothes, that was taken care of. My clothing allowance was $14 per month. I was taught to sew in order to make that small amount of clothing allowance go farther. I could find pretty scraps of fabric for fifty cents to make a little skirt. The Top Dollar Store always had sweaters on sale for a dollar. *Voila!* I had a new outfit for only $1.50! I saved every scrap of material that was left over and put it into a bag. One day, I had no money left in my monthly clothing allowance and nothing to do; I sewed the scraps all together, kind of like quilt work. Then I cut out a jumpsuit and sewed it together. I had a free garment! It probably looked tacky, but at the time I thought it was cute.

We were taken to the Baptist Church twice on Sunday. On Wednesday nights, we had prayer service at the chapel on campus, then choir practice after the prayer service. I loved to sing, so naturally, I joined the choir. We went on many choir trips while living there. When I was around the age of fifteen, the orphanage choir went on an extended tour. The kids stayed in various homes throughout the state as we traveled. It was on this choir tour that I had the extraordinary privilege to be taken on my first airplane ride. It was quite thrilling, to say the least! I remember it was during the night when we took off. I was reverent, as in having great respect for God in case we crashed; I knew I would be meeting him very soon face to face! I wanted to hang my leg out of the window of that airplane so I could touch the ground, but I knew it was too far.

These were just a few of the opportunities that I was offered while living at the orphanage. I would not have been exposed to any of these things had I stayed in the pig sty where I previously lived and only barely existed.

My first year at the orphanage, I decided that I wanted to learn to play the piano. Aunt Patty could play the piano well, and I wanted to be like her. I made an appointment to go talk to the assistant superintendent about investing in my future musical education. I went to his home, which was located next door to my cottage. When I arrived at his lovely home, he was sitting in the parlor, playing his big, beautiful pipe organ. It sounded heavenly! Oh! If only I could play as well as him and Aunt Patty! I listened intently and watched as his hands were flowing up and down both levels of the keyboards, his feet were moving back and forth, pressing the lower pedals. It really looked like a great deal of work, but I was sure I could get the hang of it if only I was given the opportunity!

After a few minutes, he stopped playing, turned around, and smiled at me in a very kind, gentle way. I timidly smiled back at him.

"Ana, I understand you want to learn to play the piano," he said in his low, soft voice.

"Yes, sir," I responded. Then I went into a nervous dissertation about how Aunt Patty could play and how she played in church. I wanted to be just like her and him. If I was only given the opportunity to take piano lessons, I promised that I would faithfully practice every day, and he would never regret having spent his money on me . . . on and on, I can't remember what all I did say, but it was the best-selling job that I could give. When I stopped talking, (or should I say, ran out of gas?), he looked at me, smiled, and said, "Ana, all you had to do was ask." With that being said, I hugged his neck, with tears of joy.

I only studied piano for three years. Then I started studying boys.

I soon learned that studying piano was much easier than studying boys! In a way, playing the piano is very much like math, in that both are an "exact science" . . . you are either right or wrong. A girl never knows when she is right or wrong when dealing with boys! They never tell you until it is too late. When reading piano sheet music, there are no grey areas. It is all there in black and white. When reading boys, there are a lot of grey areas. However, in one way, boys are a little like playing the piano. Some people can play the piano "by ear." So, I learned to simply play boys "by ear" and improvise for the rest of my school years. Boys are no Crip course!

Just when I thought I was out of my hell, I realized that boys can put a girl through another type of hell!

What type of hell you ask? Well, it's sort of like when a girl picks a daisy from a field, and she starts to pluck the petals off one by one, asking that daisy to foretell her future with a certain boy. It goes like this:

He loves me *(pluck)* . . . he loves me not *(pluck)*
He likes me *(pluck)* . . . he likes me not *(pluck)*
Will he hold my hand *(pluck)* . . . or hold it not? *(pluck)*
Will he call me *(pluck)* . . . or call me not? *(pluck)*
Will he sit by me *(pluck)* . . . or sit by me not? *(pluck)*
Will he ask me out *(pluck)* . . . or ask me not? *(pluck)*
On and on . . . you get the idea.

The answer dangles on that final petal left suspended on the stem. It's just the luck of the draw for a girl! If the final answer is not a good one, the girl can simply pick another boy, or merely pick another daisy and keep on plucking.

Boys are just plain hell to put up with sometimes!
You can't live with 'em, and you can't live with 'em!
(Yes, you read that right.)

Speaking of plucking. We had to pluck chickens twice a week at 5:30 a.m., and believe me, it was not a pleasant experience. I just couldn't eat fried chicken at night after seeing that chicken's face up close and personal that morning. I will never forget that wet, feather smell. The boys would bring around two coops of live chickens to our cottage basement. We would all go down to the basement, usually just in time to see the cook ring their necks. We watched the horrible bloody sight. I couldn't bear to see what was happening to those innocent little, squawking chickens. They were immediately dunked into hot scalding water, then the cook would hand one to each of us to pluck. Needless to say, I couldn't eat breakfast after all that!

Until her death on August 5, 1962, Marilyn Monroe was a famous, beautiful, and sexy movie star during the 1950s. She had a beauty mark on her cheek. I thought she was gorgeous, as did the rest of the world! I too had a mole on my left cheek. Since coming to the orphanage, I could now wear makeup so I decided that I would darken the mole on my cheek with my eyebrow pencil to make it look like Marilyn's. I was new to the campus, so I didn't think anyone would know the difference. It was Sunday afternoon during campus visitation time. All the kids would come to the center of the campus to visit with one another. There was a bully girl with her group of mean friends who called me over to their group. I had no idea what they wanted. I always thought the best of others, so I immediately thought they wanted to meet me and become friends. Boy was I wrong! Her name was Norma Jean, she said, "What's that on your face?" as she roughly wiped my beauty mark off my cheek with her thumb. The group laughed at me, I turned and walked away. I didn't need her as a friend, anyway.

As I was walking away, I was reminded of that old cliché:

With friends like that, who needs <u>enemas?</u>
<u>(Yes, you read that right.)</u>

The point is: Norma Jean scared the crap out of me!

I still have that mole on my left cheek. However, I don't darken it anymore. She taught me a valuable lesson that day:

<u>Don't be fake</u> (The only exception: bra forms)

The good thing about going to a new school is that you can start over with a new slate. No one knows your past. You are the new kid on the block. As always in the past, this was good for me. I always needed a new start in life. I was sort of pretty, so the cute boys wanted to get to know me, even the popular boys from town. We were from the orphanage, so they called us "home girls." It didn't take long before the popular boys found out that I was pretty but had little culture to go along with it. That was a drawback for me. I just didn't know how to act around boys. I never had a boyfriend before. In third grade, a boy asked my name, and I slapped him. He never spoke to me again. I learned that must not be the way I should respond. Well, hell! How was I to know what not to do? There was always a lot of slapping going on in my house, for one reason or another back then. . . even in cartoons!

It was about the second week of seventh grade. I got word that one of the cutest boys in eighth grade wanted to talk to me, so I agreed. He was from a wealthy family. He came over to me and started out with, "Hello there, ole chap!" I thought that was a silly and stupid first statement. I laughed and embarrassedly walked away. I didn't care how cute he was, or how wealthy his family was! I'm sorry, but that sort of talk just didn't suit my style! First impressions do matter!

About a month into my new life at the orphanage, we had recreation time one summer evening. I got word that another boy wanted to kiss me. I asked who it was, and the girl said, "Tommy." I looked over to see who he was. Hmm, he was cute, so I agreed. We met behind the recreation building. I had watched a lot of Marilyn Monroe movies, and I knew how movie stars gave movie-star kisses. I was prepared to take one. The problem was, Tommy wasn't prepared to give a movie-star kiss. We were standing behind the building with another lovebird couple for about one minute when I took charge. I pulled Tommy down and over, with me bending backward and gave him a movie-star kiss. He obviously wasn't impressed. It scared him to death! That ended that romance! I decided I must not be too good at kissing nor good at this boyfriend-girlfriend thing, so I decided to take up sports.

At first, I wasn't good at sports, but I was the meanest! I couldn't ring the basketball goal, but I could sure take the basketball away from the other players and throw it to my teammate who could shoot the goal. I could jump higher than the other girl at tip-off. No one wanted to mess with me.

At my ten-year class reunion, a classmate told me the girls were afraid of me on the basketball court in seventh grade.

Go figure! I was a wimp! I was the one that was insecure. I was only putting on a false front to keep the bullies away. Who knew?

I learned there is fame in being the best in sports. I trained myself to be the fastest runner, the highest jumper, and the strongest player in every sport.

Later in my senior year of high school, I earned The Most Physically Fit Senior Girl award.

It was November 22, 1963, and I was in seventh grade. About midway through my fifth-period math class, I was about to fall asleep with my head on my desk as I usually did, there came a knock on the door; Mrs. Dobson was handed a note. She started crying. After composing herself, she relayed the sad news to the class, "Boys and girls, they have killed the president of our United States!"

There was a gasp from all the girls, and we began to cry. Some of the boys cheered with glee. I couldn't believe how anyone could possibly be happy at a time like that! One boy said, "He's a nigger-lover anyway!" I glared at him sharply for his cruel words!

I was so somber and sad for me and for our country. I knew the pain and sorrow of losing a loved one. How could our country function without our beloved president of the United States? Again, I felt completely helpless. I worried about what would happen to me, my family, and our country without our leader. I wondered *would the communist take over our country*. I knew this would be a day that I would remember for the rest of my life!

We were immediately dismissed from school that day. I walked back to the orphanage with a big lump in my throat and a feeling of desolation for my future and for that of my younger brother and sisters. It was just now when I had gotten my life somewhat back together, after having lost my mama, and now this! I could now lose my country! I cried myself to sleep that night after having watched the television for hours upon hours of re-runs of that devastating event. We were out of school for days. To this day, no one knows definitively who, and why they killed the thirty-fifth president of the United States of America, John F. Kennedy.

Where were you the day they killed John F. Kennedy?

A bright spot in my life while living at the orphanage was that I had a pen pal. I had never had a pen pal before. Now I did, and it was my best buddy, little playmate, and big brother, Teddy. He would write to me almost weekly. I would return every letter. Sometimes, the bright spot would grow dim when he would share the news of how he was still being treated by his father, Fob. He now had it as bad as the older kids before him. At this time in his life, he was still living with Fob and Marggot (his stepmother who didn't like children). Sometimes, he would share with me about the needless whippings he was still receiving from Fob because Marggot would tell Fob that he and Tooty had been bad that day. One day, while playing in the yard, he turned over his toy dump truck; that was something his stepmother thought warranted a whipping. Fob never asked what Teddy or Tooty had done that was bad; he just whipped on demand, as he had done so many times in the past. He still loved doing the dastardly deed. Teddy was his favorite child, but even he got the bitter end of that chap belt. Only time could allow the children to outgrow Fob from using that chap belt on them.

It was 1965, and Teddy was continuing to write to me. I couldn't help but feel sorry for him. I was in eighth grade, and he was in the ninth grade. His living conditions were quite crude. He still had to use the outhouse and had to bathe in a large dishpan. It seemed that the older the house, the more Fob liked it. I guess because the houses were cheaper to rent.

Teddy wrote to me about how the boys made fun of him in gym class. Fob would not spend the money to purchase Teddy a pair of gym shorts. He was getting failing grades because he could not dress out with the class. Teddy told his coach that he couldn't dress out because his daddy would not buy him a pair of gym shorts. The coach asked for Fob to come and talk with him in hopes of settling the matter. Fob insisted that he did not have the money for gym shorts. The coach said, "Well, Mr. Waterman, do you have any pair of shorts that Teddy can wear, so he can dress out in class?" Fob said, "yes."

    The next day, Teddy showed up with a pair of cut off fatigues that Robbie had left behind, while he was home on leave from the Marines. The boys at school then started calling Teddy, "Jungle Boy."

    When Teddy was sixteen years old, he dropped out of school and started working at the local grocery store. Fob wanted him to do this, so Teddy could give him money each week. Strangely enough, the beatings stopped for Teddy at that point. Fob was nothing but a money-grubbing hellhound! However, there was a bright side to this story. With Teddy working and making his own money, he was now able to buy his own personal toilet paper! Marggot already had her own toilet paper, Teddy now could have his. Fob never bothered to use it. He always used the newspapers. Remember, Fob always said, "Waste not, want not." He never wasted the newspaper; therefore, he never wanted toilet paper.

    One summer, while I was away from the orphanage on vacation, my oldest sister Ellen took me to visit Teddy and Fob. When Ellen and I walked up to the rickety unpainted front porch, Fob walked out to meet us. The only comment Fob made to me was, "Whose baby are you?" Before I could say anything in response, he turned and walked inside. I was never invited in.

    I can truthfully say, that statement or question was the second time I ever remember Fob ever speaking to me in my whole life. I guess he knew the truth as to who my real father was, and I did not, at the time. I wonder if it hurt him to know the truth about Soldier Boy being my real father? Whoever Soldier Boy was.

Oh, well! What the hell!?

I was in the eighth grade when another devastating episode happened to me. I had finished my usual weekly chore of washing my bra forms. I always set them on top of the bathroom stall wall to dry overnight so they would be fresh for church the next Sunday morning.

The next morning, I was getting dressed to go to church, and my bra forms were missing! Horrors! Terrors! The end of the world must be happening! What on earth could have happened to my precious and most treasured bra forms? I searched for them high and low. No bra forms were to be found. No one knew what had happened to them, at least no one was admitting they knew anything. It was time to go to church, I made a quick substitute using toilet paper. That was fine, but only for a day. When a girl sweats, toilet paper begins to crumble. I had to figure a new substitute for my bra forms until I could find a way to buy another pair. However, I had never seen them in any of the local stores in town. I was in a real pickle!

Later that week, I was told that another girl had wrapped them up like a dirty Kotex and had thrown them into the garbage can! Can you imagine what a mental impact that did to me? I was ruined for life! I wondered, who could be so mean as to do such a cruel thing to such a sweet little girl such as I? Now I would have to resort to wearing bobby sox or _something_ in my bra for the rest of my life! I certainly wasn't resorting back to wearing little red potatoes in my bra. Besides, they are never the same size. I had no idea what I was going to do!

It was on a Saturday morning when the whole dormitory of us girls had to go to the Administration building. We were to attend a group therapy session with a psychologist. All fifteen of us girls arrived on time, at ten o'clock sharp. As I skeptically walked into his office and took my seat, I began to size him up. There he was, sitting behind his grey metal desk. He was an older man, sort of squatty with greasy, balding hair. His square-rimmed glasses were sitting low on his nose. I could tell if I were seated closer to him that he would probably smell of mothballs. I really did not think I would be able to relate to him, but I was willing to give him a chance anyway. He started off the session by stating that we could ask him anything and talk to him about anything that was on our minds. He said he was there to help us with any problems that we might be experiencing while living at the orphanage. No one in the group of fifteen girls said a word ... cold silence! I guess the other girls were smarter than me! I decided I would break the ice. After all, I had something on my mind that needed to be addressed!

I said, "I have a friend that wears bra forms and—"

He interrupted me, "What? Bra forms? What are bra forms? You mean falsies?"

I was so embarrassed! The whole room full of girls started snickering! They all knew what I was talking about and what I was about to say. They all knew that my friend was <u>me</u>!

I shyly lowered my head and answered his question, "Yesssss." I was trying not to show I was embarrassed by him saying the word *falsies* instead of bra forms. I wanted to appear mature; after all, I was thirteen. So, I then continued with my story of how someone had stolen my friend's bra forms and wrapped up my friend's bra forms like a dirty Kotex and had thrown them into the garbage can, and now they were gone forever! I wanted to know what he thought of that bad little girl and what punishment should happen to that bad little girl for having done that bad crime to my sweet little friend. I just knew that he would reprimand that bad little girl in the group for having done such a heinous crime. He listened intently and stared at me with a bewildered look on his face. I guess he was waiting for another remark from me or something. I had nothing else to add to the story that my sweet little friend had asked me to share with him. He then shook his head only slightly in disbelief and scribbled down a few notes. I waited patiently, tapping my foot, I just knew he was about to *lower the boom* on those bad little girls!

About that time, he raised one eyebrow, pushed his glasses back up on his greasy nose, and pursed his lips into a straight line, then he said, "Does anyone else have anything they would like to share?" **What?** I couldn't believe that was all he had to say!

I left there that day wishing I had never brought it up! I wondered, *what in the hell did he get paid for anyway?*

I was told later who the girl was that had done the dastardly, dirty deed.

On social media years later, I asked her about having done such a crime! She didn't remember anything about it! I told her that she got the blame anyway. She said she got the blame for a lot of things that she didn't do while living at the orphanage! We all did.

The house parents at the orphanage kept a close eye on all of us kids. However, with sixteen wild-ass girls all in one house, not all of them can be in your sight all the time.

Things were going to happen behind the house parent's backs, and they did. We dared not tell on one another. We would catch hell from one another if we snitched on each other.

Yes, it was a Christian upbringing. We were taken to church every Sunday morning and night. On Wednesday nights, we had prayer service at the on-campus chapel and then choir practice.

Our house parents were Christians. They lived and walked their talk. It would have been hard for anyone to dedicate their lives to taking care of a bunch of kids if they didn't have the love of Christ in their own personal lives; it took a lot of patience. As far as the things we did wrong and got caught, we were reprimanded, usually by restrictions. That meant we couldn't go to the downtown theater on the weekends, or to the football games, or to the skating rink. If we were old enough to date, we couldn't go on a date the following weekend. I had but very few dates, so this didn't affect me; but I tried to be good anyway.

One night, we were all sitting around the long dinner table, and the house parent was asking the blessing over our food. The group of girls that I was sitting with was talking during the prayer. Not me, I had my head bowed. After the blessing, the house parent told the four naughty girls that they were under restrictions. They got mad and said that I was talking during the prayer also. The house parent knew I wasn't. So, the girls decided that I must be the house parent's pet. If you have ever been in a situation where all of your friends gang up on you, you know the pain I am talking about. No one would speak to me for days. I was on kitchen duty when they were talking down to me; I was about to cry. Another girl, who wasn't really my friend at that time, looked over to me and moved her lips silently, "I want to talk to you." When we were finished with our chores, we met into the hall, and she told me that she knew I was innocent. She knew that the other girls were just mad at me because I didn't get put under restrictions with the rest of them. She said, "Don't worry about them, I will be your friend." From that moment on, Genteel Jeanine and I became friends. To this day, we are still good friends. The old saying, "A friend in need is a friend, indeed," ---So true!

In the summertime, the on-campus Olympic-size swimming pool was open six days a week for the children to enjoy. The girls could not swim at the same time as the boys, except on very special occasions. July 4 was one of those special days at the orphanage. There were all sorts of water events held on the 4th of July. I always entered the diving contests. Sometimes, I would win the swan dive. When I was older, I usually won the jackknife dive.

A group of eight girls usually entertained the large audience in mid-afternoon with synchronized swimming. We all wore one-piece bathing suits, each of different colors. We all had on rubber bathing caps, with plastic flowers that matched the color of our bathing suits. We were told that we looked pretty from a distance. I was a good swimmer, so I was asked to join the team at an early age. Being the smallest girl, I had to drag-the-tail, which meant that when we went underwater, I was the last to come up! I was good at holding my breath for long periods of time; Theo taught me to do this when I was only four years old when he would sit on my head with a pillow! As I got older, I was the leader, and I did away with that nonsense. I made the new smallest girl drag-the-tail and stay underwater longer!

The summer that I turned sixteen, I was able to take lessons to become a Red Cross lifeguard. I took both junior and senior lifeguard and passed both. I proudly wore my Red Cross, round badge on my front right leg of my white swimsuit every summer. I never had to use those useful skills, nor did I ever get a job as a lifeguard. I did, however, demonstrate my life-saving skills to any of the younger kids who were willing to let me practice on them. I still have that Red Cross badge, but I no longer wear it on any of my swimsuits today. I just look at it occasionally in my scrapbook with fond memories.

There were a lot of things that happened while living at the orphanage, both good and bad. It seems that in the long haul of time, only the bad times stand out in your mind. One of the worse things that could have ever happened to anyone happened to me when I was a junior in high school. It happened this way:

The orphanage personnel took a busload of us on a retreat to a resort in Georgia during spring break. We stayed in small groups of four in little cottages during the night; some of us were unchaperoned. We had Bible study in the daytime, along with other fun activities. One day I noticed that the absolute cutest guy on campus was flirting with me very subtly. That night, he slipped out of his cottage and came to my cottage. He asked if I might go for a walk along the lakeside with him. Of course, I did! We walked and then sat down on the sandy beach and kissed. Then we laid on the sand and kissed, and kissed, and kissed. That was all! Because I was flat-chested and wore falsies— eeer bra forms— there was no hanky-panky going on up there, nor elsewhere for that matter. Boys knew if they couldn't get past first base, they certainly couldn't make it to home plate; if you catch my drift.

The next morning, we all loaded up on the bus to head back home. I took my seat, hoping he would come and sit by me. Wrong! He walked right past me and sat with another girl. I was crushed! The whole campus knew that we had slipped out of our cottage the night before and was gone for quite some time. My reputation was ruined and for no good reason. I have no idea what he might have boasted about, or what he might have said that he might have done! Albeit, nothing did happen! Anyway, I think the other girls were simply jealous that I had the opportunity to be with the cutest guy on campus! Well, this was just the beginning of my hell!

The girls were playing up to him and flirting heavily. I had no idea what all was said behind my back from all of them, I just know there was talk. I also know that nothing really happened, other than sneaking out and kissing.

A week later, a trouble-making boy, whom we called Fatty, came up to me and said, "Athletic Athena said you had sex with John the night you slipped out with him." I immediately denied it and said it was a lie! He went straight back to Athena and told her that I called her a lying bitch. I had no idea that he was going right back to her and spread another rumor for the sole purpose of keeping trouble stirred up.

The next day, my roommate and I walked to town, as we usually did on Saturday. On the way home, we passed by Athena's cottage. A large group of girls met us mid-campus, with Athena as their leader. She was a year older, stronger, and more athletic than I. She said, "Fatty said you called me a lying bitch." I told her I didn't.

She said, "Yes—you--did!" With that being said, and before I could say another word, she hauled off and slapped the cold living hell out of me . . . right in front of everyone!

I was totally humiliated! Not only were all the rumors not true, now there was another lie on top of all that. Now, there was this humiliation of being slapped in front of everyone that I knew and thought of as friends.

All I could do was turn and walk toward my cottage, holding back my tears as best I could. I was about to explode! At that moment, I wanted to die!

When I finally made it back to my bedroom, I let it all out! I laid in my bed and cried in the darkness for hours.

As I was sobbing, I was thinking back over my life. I had been slapped before in my past life and much harder than the one I had just received. My mama was the best of the slappers; she would put Athena to shame, so could Fred. Hell! Fred knocked me out one time! Yes, there were many wicked things that I had lived through previously. Severe beatings, neglect, and molestation, to name a few. But worst of all, I never knew for sure whether I was loved. Yes, I had lived through and survived a great deal of darkness from my past. However, this one incident of humiliation in front of my friends, for some reason, tipped the iceberg! It was all I could take.

When no one knew, I slipped into the medicine closet, got a full bottle of Midol, and downed every one of them. I knew Midol was a muscle relaxer; I had hopes that it would relax my heart to the point of death. I had no reason to live.

As I was sobbing, my stomach was sloshing around the water that was filled with pills. My roommate came into our bedroom to check on me. She asked what that sloshing noise was. I was about to fall asleep, I said, "I won't have to worry about anything or anyone anymore." She knew something was wrong. She immediately told our houseparent, who in turn called the superintendent. He took me to the hospital and had my stomach pumped out. It was a horrible, gagging experience! Having that big tube stuffed down my throat and deeper into my stomach was a personal encounter that I would not wish on my worst enemy!

After the whole ordeal, the superintendent and I had a heart-to-heart talk about why I had done such a thing. I explained to him what had happened previously:

I had slipped out with John, we kissed, nothing wrong had happened. There were rumors, then lies about me, then the big slap. My reputation was ruined over nothing, other than jealousy, I guess.

The superintendent took me back to my cottage, where I rested, cried, and slept in my safe, warm bed for the duration of the night. He immediately went to Athena's cottage and spoke to all the girls. He told them what had occurred concerning me that night. He also told them my side of the story. He explained the dangers and the powers of the tongue and how deadly it can be.

James 1:26 states, "If any man among you seem to be religious, and bridleth not his tongue, but deceiveth his own heart, this man's religion is vain."

> "Even so the tongue is a little member and boasteth great things, Behold, how great a matter a little fire kindleth! And the tongue is a fire, a world of iniquity; so is the tongue among our members that it defileth the whole body, and setteth on fire the course of nature, and it is set on fire of hell." But the tongue can no man tame; it is an unruly evil, full of deadly poison. (James 3:5)

The power of the tongue said false statements about me, and the rumors had killed my reputation. My reputation was all that I had and treasured. Because of those false accusations, it led me to feel worthless and wanting to end my life. Therefore, the tongue can vicariously kill a person. The superintendent told the girls if I had been successful in ending my life that night, it would have been their fault, in an indirect way.

I think the superintendent made a point with the girls that Saturday night. I did not go to church that next morning. However, on the following Monday morning, I had to go to school. As I stepped aboard the bus, you could have heard a pin drop! Everyone knew what had happened. No one said a word to me. No one ever apologized. I just sucked it up, along with the pain and went on with life!

You know, what bullies don't realize is this: You never know what a heavy load that other person may be carrying at that time you are pushing them around. Do you really want to kill that other person? You might be a cause of death with your mean actions. Most bullies likely don't care; and if they don't care, they are probably going to hell any way.... Hum! Too bad!

God forgives us all; and all is well for me today. I am glad that I lived through that terrible ordeal in my life. God had much better plans for me later. At that time, I had no idea what. That day wasn't my time to die, and God made sure it did not happen. What I learned from that time of tribulation was this:

> *The only problem you can't solve is, getting yourself out of the grave, so don't put yourself there.*

When I was a senior in high school, I worked in a local doctor's office after school. One of the first things the office manager told me was that I was to keep everything that I learned in that office strictly confidential. That meant that if I found out someone had a specific illness; it could not leave that office! I promised complete loyalty and secrecy.

One day, the office manager called me aside and asked if a certain girl was a good girl? I said, "yes." As far as I knew, she seemed to be a good girl., by all outward appearances. Although she didn't like me and I didn't care for her, come to find out she wasn't so saintly after all. She had all of us girls fooled! That nasty little discharge she had been complaining about was gonorrhea! When I filed the test results, sure enough, there was the proof! The office manager made me swear to secrecy. I didn't tell a soul! That girl was so lucky that I didn't tell anyone! I wonder if the good doctor advised the girl that she had the dreadful disease. I guess he had to tell her because she was cured along with her partner. What is funny about the whole situation is: she never liked me! She had no idea what a big secret I was keeping to myself about her. I could have ruined her saintly reputation, but I didn't. Besides, I would have lost my job.

High school graduation day was in May 1969. I sent out several graduation invitations to family members and friends in hopes that maybe someone would be there, especially for me. Perhaps someone would be there to watch me on this proud day of my life. I proudly wore my white gown with the black cap, complete with the gold and black tassel. A little white dress and white heels were worn underneath. It was the proudest day of my life. Until now, this was my life's most significant accomplishment. I was the first in my family of ten children to graduate from high school. I did not have top honors, but I did have good grades.

I patiently waited in the long line of students before finally, my name was called---Ana Ruth Waterman Oder. I held my head up high, shoulders back, and proudly walked across the stage. I reached out and accepted that black folder, which held my diploma. The principal said, "Congratulations, Ana." I said, "Thank you," as I shook his hand. Then I walked across the stage to exit and reclaim my seat. A swell of pride and sadness made my throat tighten with a cry. I thought to myself, If Mama were alive today, I wonder if she would be proud of me and would she have attended my graduation? Then I answered my own question. I think not. She never showed an interest in any of my other activities while she was alive, why would she be interested in this? I loved her, anyway.

There were three "worse days" in my life:

1. The day my mama died; I was eleven years old. I was scared. What would happen to me? How would we survive?
2. The day I went to the orphanage and left my family, I was twelve years old. How would we like it there and get along with the other kids? How would we survive?
3. The day I left the orphanage, and I was on my own in the world at the age of seventeen. I was scared to death! How would I make a living for myself? How would I survive?

To sum up everything about living at the orphanage, I would say we all received proper nourishment, a clean, warm environment in which to live, a good education, and a Christian upbringing. Our physical needs were undoubtedly met with excellence. It was the best thing that could have ever happened to my younger siblings and me.

The only negative comment I can make about the orphanage personnel is that I was not prepared to leave the orphanage at the ripe old age of seventeen. No one ever told me what I would be good at in life. For example, No one ever said, "Ana, you like animals, you'd make a good veterinarian." Or, "Ana, you are good with the younger children, you would make a good teacher." Or, "Ana, you can fix hair, you would make a good beautician."

I had no idea what I wanted to be when I grew up, nor at what I would be good.

Finally, one person told me that I would make a good model. What do you think I pursued? During my senior year of high school, I tried out for and received a scholarship to modeling school. Being a model was not what I should have been in life. I had the grades to go to college, but I had stars in my eyes to get-rich-quick. Boy was I wrong! Why the orphanage personnel didn't encourage me to go to college is beyond my comprehension. I guess they knew I was strong-willed and high-minded, and I had my mind made up to become a model. Usually, when a person has their mind set on something, there is no changing it. I guess the orphanage personnel knew that fact about me. I am sure I would not have listened to them had they encouraged me to go to college because I was ready to get-rich-quick. You see, I thought I knew it all; but what I didn't know, was what I didn't know! I chose the wrong way to get-rich-quick back then. It was later in life that I learned:

The harder I worked, the richer I got! Go figure!

After graduation from high school, I packed everything I owned into my new piece of red Samsonite luggage, along with my new iron, which I received from the orphanage as a graduation/going-away present. Once again, I set out for another fresh start in life. This fresh start was different; it was both exciting and scary. For the first time in my life, at the age of seventeen, I was on my own, alone in the big city of Birmingham, Alabama. The superintendent of the orphanage drove me to the YWCA in Birmingham. My first month's rent was paid as well as my meal ticket. It was my responsibility to get a job and pay my expenses while attending modeling school. I looked for several days and finally landed a job working at a downtown loan office. It was near the YWCA, so I could walk to and from work each day. Modeling school was several miles away on the south side of town; so, I had to catch the bus to get there at night.

My modeling instructor took me under her wing. After all, she was the one who had faith in me to give me the scholarship. The first night at class, we were told our assignment was to read, cover to cover, Amy Vanderbilt's *Book of Etiquette* before the end of the course. I didn't have the money to buy the book, nor did I have a library card. I was lucky, Mrs. Nelson let me borrow her book. The book was about two and a half inches thick. How was I to read that? I worked all day! I dared not to read it, for she would surely know! We were quizzed on various parts of the book from time to time. I was so glad I took the time to read that book. It helped me then and later in life. I still rely on it.

Modeling class ended around ten each night. After class, Mrs. Nelson sometimes took me around the corner to a local diner and bought my dinner before taking me back home to the YWCA. This was our time together that she could mentor me. She knew that I was from the orphanage and was not exposed to anything in the world! One of the most valuable personal lessons that she shared with me was this:

"If you lie down with the pigs, you'll get up smelling like them."

I really didn't get what she was talking about altogether. She tried to explain to me that Birmingham was a big city and a young, naive girl, like myself, could get into trouble quickly if she wasn't careful. With absolutely no supervision and guidance, there were plenty of men who would take advantage of me. I was sure to watch out for those pigs from then on.

It seemed like no time, and I had finished modeling school. Now what? I still wasn't getting those calls to come and model. Saturday morning runway jobs at local department stores seemed to be all I could get. I was an ingénue model. I wasn't quite tall enough to be a high fashion model; therefore, I never made it big time. I liked modeling, but the pay wasn't great! I did, however, get a discount on the clothing from the department stores. Those stars in my eyes faded away because I wasn't making those big bucks that I had hoped for. I didn't have the money to be seen in the right places, with the right people, at the right time. I didn't have the money needed for that all-important photo portfolio.

So, I got a real, paying job.

Later in life, I entered college and paid for my higher education myself.

My next job, I started out working in the advertising department for a large corporation in downtown Birmingham. I was on my new job for only two weeks when one of the top managers in the head office lost his secretary, who got mad and quit. He was told by the personnel manager that I had secretarial skills. He asked if I might fill-in until he could hire another executive secretary. I joyfully said, "Yes!" After two more weeks, he liked me and saw that I could do the job. He asked if I would like to have the position as his executive secretary. Of course, I again said yes, followed by, "Does this mean I will get a pay raise?" He smiled, laughed and said, "Well, I will see, but if you do get a raise, it will be the first and fastest raise this company has ever given an employee."

I got the raise. God just dumped that great job into my lap! Finally, someone was looking out for me! I think God was looking out for me all along, and I just didn't know it. I worked there for two years and loved every minute of it. It was a swanky office with glamorous appeal. I sat behind a big mahogany desk with an electric typewriter, which I could operate quite superbly. A large board room was to my right with a thirty-foot long mahogany table. Beautiful artful, marble ashtrays graced the center of the table. Fresh flowers and cold-water pitchers were placed there during meetings. Coffee was served in the corner of the room. At the front of the room was a large pull-down screen where my boss presented his monthly report and financial projections. One of my responsibilities was to prepare his presentation each month from his notes.

I was working alongside high, powerful men who respected me and my position. My work was essential for them to look good and be successful in their jobs. I felt, for the first time in my life, I was indeed an essential and valued person! The pay was great also! I should have never quit that fantastic job, but I got married, and my new husband wanted me to stop working and stay at home. So, I did.

14.
Life after Death

As I am finishing this little book, an odd thing occurred to me: sequences of time happened in elevens:
Fob was eleven years older than Mama.
Mama was eleven years older than Fred.
Fred was a few months scant of being eleven years older than Opee.
Opee was eleven years older than me.
I was eleven years old when Mama died.
It was eleven years later when I got my answer as to "Why?"

A few years had passed, and I had grown up a bit. I slowly stopped my modeling career and had worked as an executive secretary for a large corporation. Now that too had ended. I now found myself married and living in a suburban neighborhood of Birmingham, Alabama.

I was sitting in the kitchen of my new home one delightful, sun-shiny morning on August 19, 1973. I was feeding my beautiful baby boy his breakfast of the usual fruit, oatmeal, and milk. He was only six months of age. As I lovingly looked into the face of this precious child of mine, a cry started swelling up within my throat. I realized that day was exactly eleven years to the date that my mama had died. I started drowning in self-pity, remembering the pain of losing my mother on that fateful morning. I was crying for that little girl who was hurt so badly; the little girl who was feeling so lost, empty, and helpless on that day so long ago. The little girl who was sitting in the treetop on that Sunday morning, crying, mad at God, and questioning, "Why did you take my mama?"

Well, that little girl no longer exists; however, the pain of those old memories remains plastered on my heart. I will always secretly cry for that little girl who was so deeply hurt long ago.

While sitting there feeding and adoring my pretty little son, I was thinking, *my beautiful baby boy would never have the blessing of a loving grandmother.* He would never be able to sit on a grandmother's knee and be rocked to sleep or have her sing a lullaby to him. No, he would never have any of these beautiful blessings because God had taken my mother away from me. Although my mama would have never been that type of grandmother to my son, I was still hurting for his loss.

About that time, I felt the warm spew of oatmeal across my face. My beautiful baby boy had spat the whole mouthful of his breakfast onto my face and was laughing gleefully! His little cheeks were pinched upward with his little dimples were showing, and his eyes were sparkling in the sunlight. My tears of self-pity immediately turned into laughter along with his. We laughed, and I cried and laughed more for what seemed like a long time, as I hugged him tightly and kissed his pretty little baby face.

It was at that moment that God revealed to me the answer to that old question I had asked so many times for the past eleven years: "God, why did you take my mama?" I was so young; I needed my mama.

God had taken my mama out of my life for me to have a better way in life. Had she not died, I would have continued to live in poverty, remained in ignorance, and nothing would have changed, the vicious cycle would have continued. Instead, look at me today, I was taken away from all that hell and degradation. At the orphanage, I was given the opportunity to obtain a good education, a great Christian nurturing and upbringing. I was taught to seek a higher standard and a better way of living. I was taught to set my goals for excellence. All these virtues I would have never been exposed to had I stayed in the crude, nasty, poverty-stricken surroundings in which we were living.

Ignorance begets ignorance.

Mama's dying stopped that deteriorating chain reaction of events.

God knew that he had a better plan for my life. It was not for me to live the rest of my life in a hell hole pigsty.

It was now my time to give that love, guidance, support, and protection to my child. More importantly, it was my responsibility to teach my son about our Heavenly Father and how he loves us much more than we can ever imagine or understand. I must teach my son that we must ultimately look to God our Father for love, guidance, support, and protection. I knew if I could instill all that into my son as a young child, he would grow up to be a godly man.

"Train up a child in the way he should go; even when he is old, he will not depart from it" (Prov. 22:6).

As a Christian parent, it was my responsibility to teach my son that Jesus should be the center of his life. Therefore, I must be the Christlike role model whom he would want to mimic.

I knew that to be that type of role model would be tough and overwhelming at times, so I stopped and thanked God for his infinite love for me. I prayed that I would be the type of parent who would be pleasing to him. I asked for his careful hand to guide me throughout the process of rearing my child.

I had to stop looking back at my past sad circumstances and past failures that were holding me down. I now realized God was there with me during all those dark days and bad times. Surely, I could trust him with my future today. I just needed to keep my eyes focused on him. He had done an excellent job of protecting me so far. The word *trust* kept coming into my thoughts.

The circle of life is a mysterious thing. We come into this world, stay for a fleeting moment, then *poof*, we are gone. Then someone else is left to carry on in our place. Will they remember you? Yes, but only for a short time. Just like my mama—one day she was here, then suddenly gone. After she died, it was then my time to carry on, even when I didn't think I could.

When I have vanished from this earth, gone on to be with the Heavenly Father, it is my hope and prayer that my child will look back with fond memories and say that his mother taught him and led him to know the Lord. If he can say that, then my life on this earth will have been worth it all. Until then, I will continue to ask: What are you passing on to the loved ones in your circle?

My name is Ana, and that was my story. I lived through it, and I am stronger today because God was with me all the way even when I didn't know it.

Yes, I was *Born into Hell*, but I am now Heaven bound!

Epilogue

Various circumstances have caused the family to disburse in different directions. Some siblings just plainly do not like one another, so why bother to keep in touch?

When the four little ones were placed into the orphanage, they slowly lost contact with the six older ones. The siblings grew apart and went their separate ways in life. After much effort on the part of the ones who cared, some brothers and sisters were reunited later in life.

Opee, Teddy, Ana, and Junior were reunited at an extended family reunion a few years ago. They began to share old family stories. Teddy and Ana remember the last week of Mama's life from a child's perspective. Junior barely remembers her, for he was just six years old. However, Opee was an adult when Mama died, and he had some very enlightening information to share about the last two weeks of Mama's life. None of the younger ones remember the events leading up to her illness. The only thing they remembered was that she started getting sick, then she abruptly died.

In the words of Opee

Sometimes I think back on those two weeks before Mama died and remember that Mama, Fred, and I planned to go to the Grand Olé Opry in the middle of August. It would be one of those Po' folks mini-vacations, i.e., leave on a Saturday morning, go to the Opry that evening, stay in a motel Saturday night, and drive back all day Sunday.

We were looking forward to the trip, or at least, Fred and I were. A week before the date, out of the blue Mama told us, "You and Fred have women to take with you. You don't want me to go with you!"

It did no good to try and talk any sense into her. This wasn't her first time to adopt that attitude. It was like she wanted us to beg her to go. I think the best word to describe her would be recalcitrant.

Until today, I believe she changed her mind about going and didn't want to come right out and say it. By saying that Fred and I had girlfriends on the side, she could convince us that she would not be going, then she thought we would cancel the trip.

Fred and I talked it over. We figured that either Mama had lost interest in going or she wanted us to beg her to go. We decided to tell Mama we would go by ourselves if she didn't want to go. So that is what we told her, and she didn't like it.

Mama visited Ellen a few days before she got sick and told her, "Fred and Opee think they are going to the Grand Ole' Opry next week, but I'm going to make sure they don't go."

It was a few days after that visit with Ellen when Mama became very sick. Within a week, she was dead.

I think until the day Ellen died, she thought and believed that Mama drank something that would make her sick so we would have pity on her and not go on our trip. Maybe Mama didn't mean to kill herself, but she messed up and drank too much, and it did kill her. Who knows?

I wouldn't put it past her to have done something like that to stop us from making the trip. But why? All she had to do was go along with the plan that we had put in place a month earlier.

Maybe she did nothing at all. Perhaps she really did have ESP, and she felt as if something was about to happen. Or maybe it was just her time to go and get out of her hell.

I guess we will never know, for now.

Ana's comments

What a shame that Mama lived her life, died so young, and had nothing good to show for it. She left behind ten broken-down children. She left nothing good to pass on to them. Mama never taught her children to love the Lord, for she did not know the Lord, so, how could she?

"Behold, children are a heritage from the Lord."
(Ps. 127:3).

"Children obey your parents in the Lord; for this is right. Honor thy father and mother; which is the first commandment with promise. That it may be well with thee, and thou mayest live long on the earth. And ye fathers, provoke not your children to wrath: but bring them up in the nurture and admonition of the Lord."
(Eph. 6:1–4).

We children did our part. We obeyed, not out of love but out of fear of beatings. We all outlived our parents.
Our parents failed on their part to bring us up in the admonition of the Lord.
If Mama had only known the Lord, she could have made a world of difference in all our young lives back then. It would have made it so much better for us even so today.

Goodbye from Me to You

Yes, we survived *child abuse* to the ultimate use of those two words. Although we will never forget the excruciating pain of our past, some of us have become *victors* and have decided to make good things out of the bad that happened to us.

Did it make us *better people today*? I don't know.

Did it make us *stronger* today? I think yes!

Yes, we children were *victims*.

It is our choice whether to become *victimizers* today.

We can become *victors* if we choose to be.

The vicious cycle ended with some of us. Some did not have the opportunities offered to me.

If you or anyone you know are in an abusive situation, act now! Go tell someone before it is too late. There is help there for you… it is only a computer's Google away!

It is my hope that maybe someone, somewhere, who has had the unfortunate experience that we had will read this little book and see that there is hope for a brighter tomorrow.

No, we can't change our past, but we can change how we look at life and take charge of our future.

Tenacity, my friend,

Tenacity!

Your average little girl,

Ana Waterman

Today

Opee lives a quiet life with his loving wife Sundee in a small town in lower Alabama. He is a retired professional from law enforcement after many years of service. They love and enjoy the frequent visits of their children and grandchildren. He is a silent philanthropist to the less fortunate.

Teddy went back to school and received his GED with honors later in life. He is retired and lives a millionaire's life. No one would ever know this if they met him on the street.

Ana had only the one child whom she calls "Sonshine." She resides in a small town near Opee and Teddy. After a career in business, she and her husband Ralph are enjoying a loving, peaceful life together. Life should be this good for everyone.

Junior lives a peaceful, comfortable life in mid-state Alabama and works for the state. He never got married. He calls his two dogs his children, and they are treated better than we were.

P. S. Many years later, DNA tests proved that Ana indeed is not a full sibling to the others. Fob nor Fred was neither Ana's father. Soldier Boy must have been her real father, after all. I wish I had known him.

www.ingramcontent.com/pod-product-compliance
Lightning Source LLC
Chambersburg PA
CBHW021405290426
44108CB00010B/394